UNDERSTANDING THE AMERICANS WITH DISABILITIES ACT

SECOND EDITION

WILLIAM D. GOREN

AMERICAN BAR ASSOCIATION
Defending Liberty
Pursuing Justice

GP|Solo
ABA General Practice, Solo & Small Firm Section

Cover design by ABA Publishing

10 09 08 07 06   5 4 3 2 1

Cataloging-in-Publication data is on file with the Library of Congress

Americans with Disabilities Act, Second Edition / Goren, William
    ISBN: 978-1-59031-765-5

Discounts are available for books ordered in bulk. Special consideration is given to state bars, CLE programs, and other bar-related organizations. Inquire at Book Publishing, ABA Publishing, American Bar Association, 321 North Clark Street, Chicago, Illinois 60610.

www.ababooks.org

Contents

Preface

There is a saying that if you are going to write a book, do it because you have to. Any other motive just won't lead to the necessary satisfaction. I *had* to write this update for several reasons.

First, while there are many Americans with Disabilities Act (ADA) tomes on the market, I still have not seen any books devoted exclusively to the ADA, besides the first edition of this book, that attempt to make the ADA understandable in an easy-to-use way.

Second, I saw a need for an ADA book that was written from the perspective of a lawyer with a disability (I was born with a severe to profound hearing loss and wear hearing aids). To me, the Americans with Disabilities Act is not just a law, but a way of life. For example, in this book we will discuss the concept of reasonable accommodations. Two examples of reasonable accommodations I ask for every day of my life are: 1) asking people on the phone to give examples of the letters they are saying (*c* as in *cat*, *p* as in *Patrick*), because without being able to read lips—an impossibility on the phone—I am unable to understand what letter is meant; and 2) asking people not to cover their mouth with their hands. You can't read lips with something obscuring the mouth. Both of these are examples of reasonable accommodations.

Third, I saw a need for an ADA book that discussed preventive lawyering with regard to the ADA.

Fourth, in all my dealings with the ADA over the years, I have been disappointed with the level of ADA knowledge beyond that held by certain members of the defense bar, though I have been very encouraged that there are, as of this writing, plaintiff attorneys willing to take on ADA matters and do a good job of it. I thought if I could write a book that clarified the ADA, more people would have a better understanding of just what the ADA is and is not. Only then will the ADA get beyond the myths to become a workable and desirable law.

Fifth, since the first edition was published, the U.S. Supreme Court has decided over a dozen cases on the ADA. There have also been many appellate decisions. While it has been heartening to see the book maintain its currency for the most part through these decisions, the Supreme Court decisions not included in the first book and some of the appellate opinions that have come down since then must be analyzed if the reader is to understand the workings of the ADA as it exists today. Thus, some topics that were in the first edition have been dropped, while other topics have been added. Also, many of the topics that were in the first edition have been expanded upon with new case law. Thus, you will find well over 350 new end notes in this edition that were not in the first edition. In short, a road map is fine, but the map has to be accurate.

With these goals in mind, a couple of warnings are in order. First, the ADA is an extremely broad and comprehensive law. This book is not a treatise and is not meant to address every contingency that can arise. Rather, the book highlights various aspects of the ADA so that by the end, the reader will have an excellent overview of the law, as well as a framework for dealing with it in a preventive manner. Second, the ADA is constantly changing; there are new developments every day. Thus, when an ADA issue arises, it is critical that the reader consult a lawyer knowledgeable about the area of the ADA that you are involved with. Finally, keep in mind that the cases cited in this book are for illustrative purposes only and are not meant to substitute for expert legal advice. A lawyer knowledgeable about the ADA should be consulted for the reader's specific legal needs.

William D. Goren

Acknowledgments

I want to dedicate this edition of the book to my wife, Susan, for encouraging me to write this update and for all her support in so many ways. I would also like to dedicate this book to the newest addition to our family, my daughter, Maya, for enriching my life in ways I could never imagine. I also want to acknowledge the following people for their assistance with ensuring that the ADA forms were current and user-friendly for the practitioner: Charles L. Thompson IV, a partner in the San Francisco office of the Labor and Employment Management law firm of Kauf, McClain and McGuire; and Howard Rosenblum, an attorney with the disability rights advocacy group Equip for Equality, in Chicago, Illinois, and long-time chairman of the Midwest Center for the Law and Deaf. Lastly, I wanted to thank Richard G. Paszkiet, Executive Editor, ABA Publishing, for his unflagging support, patience, and enthusiasm for this project.

William D. Goren

About the Author

William D. Goren is an associate professor of legal studies at Northwestern Business College's Naperville, Illinois, campus, where he has won numerous teaching awards. A member of the Illinois and Texas bars, Mr. Goren has published and presented widely on disability rights, employment law, health law, constitutional law, sports law, contracts, and preventive law. Mr. Goren has an A.B. from Vassar College, a J.D. from the University of San Diego, and an LL.M. in health law from DePaul University.

Concepts Underlying the ADA and Key Definitions

1

CONCEPTS UNDERLYING THE ADA

WHEN DEALING WITH the Americans with Disabilities Act (ADA), it is important to understand the concepts behind it and why the law was enacted. One reason it was enacted was the extreme cost to the federal government of supporting people with disabilities who could be productive members of the work force. In fact, it has been estimated that the inability of people with disabilities to work costs the United States $111.6 billion every year in medical costs and lost wages.

It is important to discuss the fundamental premise behind the ADA in order to prevent confusion when it comes to applying the law. The ADA is not an affirmative action statute. Instead, its purpose is to enable people with disabilities to be placed at the same "starting line" as those who are nondisabled. The Equal Opportunity Employment Commission's (EEOC's) phrase is "equal opportunity to attain the same level of performance as his/her colleagues."[1] In the workplace, it is then up to the employee to demonstrate what he or she can do. In the context of using governmental programs and places of public accommodations, getting the person with a disability to the same starting line gives him or her the opportunity to take advantage of the same services, activities, and businesses everyone else uses.

The starting-line analogy is useful in other respects as well. Plaintiff advocates should find it very helpful, since it appeals to Americans' sense of fair play. This concept also works very well in educating employees about accommodating a person with a disability. It is quite common for a person without a disability to believe that a person with a disability who is being accommodated is obtaining some sort of advantage. A true reasonable accommodation does no such thing. It simply gives the person with a disability an equal chance by putting all employees at the same starting line.

Finally, the reader needs to keep in mind that the ADA is an extremely broad law. It affects almost all areas of the legal universe in some way. The ADA applies to private employers of fifteen or more employees, nonfederal governmental entities of any size, and places of public accommodations. There are also provisions applying to transportation relay systems for the deaf and certain miscellaneous provisions. I am not aware of much controversy with respect to these other provisions, and thus they are not a subject for this book.

KEY DEFINITIONS

Because the ADA deals with discrimination against persons with disabilities, perhaps the key definition is that of the word *disability*. When people think of disabilities, they generally think of persons in wheelchairs or with severe vision impairments. However, the definition of disability under the ADA is far broader. A person has a disability under the ADA if he or she:

- has a physical or mental impairment *that substantially limits* one or more of life's major activities;
- has a record of such an impairment regardless of whether he or she currently is substantially limited in a major life activity; or
- is perceived as having such an impairment.[2]

The definitions of disability mentioned above, however, are not as straightforward as they appear. The term *substantially limits* according to the EEOC refers to an individual who is unable to perform, or is significantly limited in the ability to perform, an activity an average person in the general population can perform.[3] Under this theory, a person who is deaf does not have the ability to hear compared to an average person, so the person who cannot hear has a disability. However, a strong argument can be made that the U.S. Supreme Court's decision in *Toyota Motor Mfg., Kentucky, Inc. v. Williams*[4] superseded the EEOC regulations on this issue. In *Toyota Motor Mfg., Kentucky, Inc. v. Williams,* the plaintiff worked at a manufacturing plant in Georgetown, Kentucky.[5] She was eventually placed on an engine fabrication assembly line, where her duties included work with pneumatic tools.[6] Using the pneumatic tools caused pain in the plaintiff's hands, wrists, and arms.[7] The plaintiff then sought treatment at Toyota's in-house medical service, where she was diagnosed with bilateral carpal tunnel syndrome and bilateral tendonitis.[8]

For the next two years, Toyota put the plaintiff on various modified duty jobs.[9] These jobs did not go as the plaintiff planned, and she filed both a worker's compensation and an ADA suit, both of which were settled.[10] After these lawsuits, she returned to work at Toyota and was placed on a team in quality control inspection operations.[11] The quality control inspection operation team had four tasks: 1) assembly paint; 2) paint second inspection; 3) shell body audit; and 4) ED surface repair.[12] For the next couple of years, the plaintiff worked in assembly paint and paint second inspection.[13] The plaintiff and Toyota subsequently agreed that she was physically capable of performing the assembly paint and paint second inspection jobs.[14] During the fall of 1996, Toyota announced that all quality control inspection operation team members had to rotate through all four quality control inspection operation tasks.[15] Having to perform all of these tasks led to the plaintiff being diagnosed with other medical conditions.[16] This in turn led to a dispute over accommodations and eventually resulted in termination of her employment.[17] The plaintiff then filed a charge of disability discrimination with the EEOC and, after receiving her right to sue letter, filed suit in federal court.[18] The plaintiff alleged that she was substantially limited in several different life activities, among them manual tasks.[19]

The U.S. Supreme Court had two issues before it. For purposes of this specific discussion, the Court was faced with the question of what it means to be substantially limited in a major life activity. As noted above, the EEOC had already formulated its own definition of what *substantially limits* means, and the Supreme Court acknowledged as much in its decision. [20] However, the Court said the EEOC regulations were silent when it came to determining what *substantial limitations in performing manual tasks* meant.[21] Thus, the Supreme Court turned to standard dictionaries to help it answer the question and decided that to be substantially limited in performing manual tasks meant that the person had to have to have an impairment that prevented or severely restricted the individual from performing manual tasks.[22] So, we now know that, at least with respect to performing manual tasks, "substantially limits" refers to whether a person is *prevented or severely restricted*. What we don't know is whether this definition can be extended to all major life activities. If *Toyota Motor* is not extended across the board, then you have one set of rules for all major life activities except working and another for the major life activity of performing manual tasks. It seems rather odd that a U.S. Supreme Court case could limit itself to setting forth standards that apply only when the major life activity of performing manual tasks is alleged rather than major life activities in general. On the other hand, failure to limit *Toyota Motor* to performing manual tasks has the result of significantly limiting the scope of the ADA by eliminating from the Act's protections many persons who would otherwise be covered.

While at first glance it may be hard to believe that the definition of *substantial limitation on a major life activity* varies depending on the major life activity at issue, nevertheless, some courts are limiting *Toyota Motor* to its facts. One such case is *EEOC v. Sears*, from the Seventh Circuit, decided on August 10, 2005.[23] In *Sears*, the EEOC sued on behalf of a plaintiff (the plaintiff intervened in the suit brought by the EEOC) suffering from neuropathy and non-insulin-dependent diabetes.[24] The result of these conditions was that the plaintiff, Keane, eventually could no longer walk the equivalent of one city block without her right leg and feet becoming numb.[25] When that happened, walking became virtually impossible and extremely slow.[26] The plaintiff felt as if she would have to use her hands to lift up her leg to take one step at a time.[27] Sometimes the plaintiff doubted whether she could make it out of her worksite safely and would have to hold onto the wall for support.[28] The lower court granted summary judgment for the defendant and Keane appealed.[29] The Seventh Circuit disagreed with the lower court grant of summary judgment on whether Keane had a disability under the ADA and remanded it back to the lower court for further proceedings.[30] After the case had been remanded back to the lower court, *Toyota Motor* was decided by the U.S. Supreme Court.[31] The lower court then revisited the issue of whether Keane had a disability under the ADA and concluded that the *Toyota Motor* standard for what constitutes a substantial limitation on a major life activity was not met by Keane; therefore, Keane did not have a disability protected by the ADA.[32] The case was once again appealed to the Seventh Circuit.[33] The Seventh Circuit in the second appeal was faced with two issues: first, whether *Toyota Motor* was the proper standard to use in determining whether Keane was substantially limited in a major life activity under the ADA,[34] and second, whether Sears could be liable for refusing to accommodate Keane, assuming Keane was a person with a disability under the ADA.[35] We will explore the second issue later in this book.

Returning to the first issue, whether Keane was substantially limited in a major life activity under the ADA, the Seventh Circuit reversed the lower court's summary judgment for defendant and reasoned as follows. First, the Seventh Circuit noted that in the *Toyota Motor* decision, both parties assumed that the EEOC regulations defining *substantially limits* were reasonable; therefore, the Court had no occasion to decide the level of deference due the regulations.[36] Second, the Seventh Circuit believed the phrasing of the Supreme Court's reasoning in *Toyota Motor* was such that the Court was limiting its decision to the major life activity of performing manual tasks.[37] Third, the Seventh Circuit noted that even after *Toyota Motor*, many other Circuits had reached the conclusion that the EEOC definition of *substantially limits* was still useful guidance.[38] Fourth, the Seventh Circuit noted that the Supreme Court in *Toyota Motor* expressly limited its grant of certiorari to the question of whether the plaintiff in that case was substantially limited in the major life activity of performing manual tasks.[39] Finally, the Seventh Circuit noted that the Supreme Court in *Toyota Motor* focused on manual tasks that the plaintiff could perform as part of the basis for its decision.[40] All of the aforementioned reasons led a panel of the Seventh Circuit to conclude that considerably more flexibility exists for a plaintiff when it comes to determining whether a substantial limitation on a major life activity exists where that major life activity is anything else besides performing manual tasks.[41]

It is really not possible to discuss "substantially limits" without also discussing "major life activity." The EEOC never really defined what a major life activity was; it just gave examples.[42] In *Toyota Motor*, the Supreme Court also discussed what defines a major life activity. The Supreme Court held that a major life activity is any activity of central importance to most people's daily lives.[43]

If a person takes medicine or uses prosthetic devices to compensate for a disability, does that make the person no longer disabled under the ADA? For example, is a person who has a hearing loss and wears hearing aids not disabled under the ADA? It can be argued that, with the rare exception of fully correctable vision,[44] a prosthetic device allows a person with a disability to *compensate* for the disability rather than cure it. For example, does a person with a substantial hearing loss who wears hearing aids and reads lips have a disability under the ADA? What if a person with 20/200 vision wears glasses, which correct her vision to 20/20 or better: does that person have a disability? I was born with a 65-90 dB hearing loss in both ears, which is in the severe to profound hearing loss range. However, I have always worn top-of-the-line hearing aids, read lips, and, through hard work on my own, have excellent rhetorical skills. Do I have a disability? Certainly, absent the hearing aids, I most certainly do; however, I wear my hearing aids all the time except when I am in the shower or sleeping.

To answer this question, it bears discussing several U.S. Supreme Court cases. The leading case on mitigating measures was decided June 22, 1999, by the U.S. Supreme Court in *Sutton v. United Airlines.*[45] In *Sutton,* twin sisters applied to be commercial airline pilots for United Airlines.[46] United Airlines, while admitting the sisters had the requisite credentials, did not hire them, because under United's rules all pilots had to have uncorrected vision of not more than 20/100.[47] The twin sisters' uncorrected vision was 20/200 in one eye and 20/400 in the other.[48] United Airlines maintained that the term "substantially limits a major life activity" meant that the substantial limitation actually and presently existed.[49] United also claimed that disregarding mitigating measures taken by an individual defied the statutory command that the ADA is an individually based act.[50]

Writing for the Court, Justice O'Connor was persuaded by United's position and held that the ADA as a whole required that the positive and negative effects of mitigating measures used by a person with a disability must be taken into account in determining whether a plaintiff is substantially limited in a major life activity and was thus disabled under the ADA.[51] Justice O'Connor reached this conclusion in the following manner:

First, the phrase "substantially limits" appears in the ADA in the present indicative verb form.[52] Thus, writing for the Court, she believed that the language is properly read to require a person to be presently, and not potentially or hypothetically, substantially limited in order to demonstrate a disability.[53] In other words, a disability exists only where an impairment substantially limits a major life activity and not where it might, could, or would be a substantial limitation if mitigating measures were not taken.[54]

Second, refusing to consider the positive and negative effects of mitigating measures runs directly against the ADA's mandate to consider every individual with a disability on his or her own terms.[55]

Third, refusing to consider the negative and positive effects of mitigating measures also leads, in Justice O'Connor's view, to the bizarre conclusion that the result of medications, even if severe, could not be considered in determining whether a person has a disability.[56]

Fourth, Justice O'Connor as well as some of the other justices, particularly Justice Ginsburg in her concurrence, makes a great deal of the fact that Congress in its findings said that 43 million people were disabled. If mitigating measures were included in this figure, then surely the number would have been much higher.[57] This is a curious argument, especially when it is combined with *Toyota Motor*, discussed above. If you define *substantially limits* as prevents or severely restricts and you then factor in the inclusion of mitigating measures per *Sutton*, it would seem that Congress very much overestimated the number of persons with disabilities with its 43 million figure.

Finally, Justice O'Connor in her opinion states that an employer is free to decide that physical characteristics or medical conditions that do not rise to the level of an impairment are preferable to others, just as it can decide that some limiting, but not substantially limiting (presumably taking mitigating measures into account), impairments make individuals less than ideally suited for the job.[58]

Justice Stevens wrote a dissenting opinion in which Justice Breyer joined; Justice Breyer also wrote a separate opinion. Justice Stevens in his opinion was convinced that mitigating measures should not be considered in determining whether a person with a disability is disabled under the ADA. He reasoned as follows:

First, due to the remedial purpose of the ADA, Justice Stevens believed that the ADA should be given a generous rather than miserly construction.[59]

Second, Justice Stevens noted that eight of the nine Circuits that had considered the issue had decided against considering mitigating measures as part of the calculus for determining a disability under the ADA. [60]

Third, as we have discussed previously, the ADA has three different ways to determine whether a person has a disability. Justice Stevens believed that the sweep of those definitions meant that Congress intended to cover persons with disabilities in their unmitigated state as disabled under the ADA.[61]

Fourth, Justice Stevens said that considering mitigating measures means that a person's safeguards as a person with a disability vanish when the person makes him- or herself more employable by ascertaining ways to overcome his or her physical or mental disabilities.[62]

Fifth, Justice Stevens spent considerable time in his dissent going over the legislative and regulatory history of the ADA, which, in his view, unambiguously shows that the policy makers intended to cover disabilities in their unmitigated state.[63]

Sixth, Justice Stevens did not put much stock in the 43 million figure of persons with disabilities because he notes that the Supreme Court has in the past said that certain laws are broader than they originally appear to be, such as the case where they decided that male-on-male harassment is actionable.[64]

Seventh, Justice Stevens flat-out disagreed with Justice O'Connor's assertion about the flexibility employers have in establishing job requirements. Justice Stevens says in his opinion that it is eminently sensible and consistent with the purpose of the ADA to require employers making hiring and firing decisions based on an individual's uncorrected vision to clarify why having such a requirement is valid.[65] One wonders if the reason the Court never considered whether the uncorrected vision requirement was "kosher" was because the case was structured so that the major life activity argued as being limited was working and not seeing.

Eighth, including mitigating measures is not appropriate, according to Justice Stevens, because it ignores the fact that persons with disabilities face stereotyping regardless of whether they use mitigating measures, and the ADA was meant to help eliminate those stereotypes.[66]

Finally, Justice Stevens believed that if mitigating measures were included, it was entirely possible that people within the core group of the 43 million disabled would not be protected.[67]

Justice Breyer wrote a concurring opinion in which he said that the choice was between including some persons that Congress may not have intended to include versus excluding persons Congress definitely intended to include. Faced with that choice, he agreed with Justice Stevens for the reasons discussed above and would have held that mitigating measures should not be considered in determining whether a person has a disability under the ADA.[68]

So where does this leave us regarding mitigating measures? On a personal level, do I have a disability after all this? The answer is, who knows? because of the *Toyota Motor* case. If you recall from a previous discussion, a strong argument can be made that "substantially limiting in the major life activity" refers to whether a person is prevented or severely restricted from performing that major life activity regardless of the life activity alleged.[69] Thus, the combination of *Sutton* and *Toyota Motor* creates a disincentive for the person with a disability to use mitigating measures. The whole idea of using mitigating measures is to compensate for that disability so that the person can function close to the way the nondisabled person does. However, if mitigating measures work, then by definition a person who uses mitigating measures would not be prevented from or severely restricted in performing a major life activity. To discourage people with disabilities from using mitigating measures would seem to be bad public policy. However, it is a conclusion compelled by a reading of *Sutton* and *Toyota Motor*.

Finally, under *Sutton* and *Toyota Motor*, it is entirely possible that persons with a physical impairment using mitigating measures may be protected under the ADA depending on the time of day or the circumstances in which they find themselves. For example, a person with a hearing impairment who uses hearing aids may or may not, depending on the nature of his or her hearing loss, be disabled under the ADA while he or she wears the hearing aid(s). However, people who wear hearing aids do not wear them all the time. Even people who do wear hearing aids often, such as myself, will take them off when they shower or when they go to sleep. Thus, during those times a person is not wearing hearing aid(s), that person would most definitely have a disability under the ADA. Accordingly, a person with a hearing impair-

ment who wears hearing aids and has a job that requires staying over-
night, whether it be in a hotel or a residential facility, would be entitled
to various accommodations, such as a flashing light for an alarm clock,
flashing smoke alarm, flashing door knock, etc., but may or may not
be entitled to reasonable accommodations during the day depending
on the severity of the loss and the type of hearing aids he or she wears.
Such a conclusion may not have been intended by *Sutton* and *Toyota
Motor,* but nevertheless follows quite logically from the holdings of
those cases.

One of the ironies of *Sutton* is that a person who wears hearing
aids is going to have a harder time proving that he or she is covered by
the ADA than a person of the same hearing loss who has decided for
whatever reason not to wear hearing aids.[70] The irony is even greater
when one considers that the person who wears hearing aids, regardless
of the actual loss, is more likely to consider himself disabled than the
person who does not wear hearing aids, particularly if those considering themselves culturally deaf are factored in.

What tips can the practitioner gain from this discussion? For start-
ers, the lawyer should ascertain whether a plaintiff uses mitigating
measures. If the answer is yes, it is quite possible that the lawyer will
need to get expert medical testimony as to why the mitigating measures used by the person at issue prevent or severely restrict the person
from performing the major life activity alleged or that the mitigating
measures keep the plaintiff from performing certain major life activities when compared to the average person. [71]

Before leaving the discussion of "substantially limits," the case of
Albertsons, Inc. v. Kirkingburg[72] should be discussed. In that case,
Albertsons hired the plaintiff to drive a truck.[73] Kirkingburg had more
than a decade of driving experience at the time he was hired and had
performed well.[74] He passed the vision test prior to hiring on at
Albertsons.[75] He had no problems driving for Albertsons, but unfortunately suffered an injury.[76] In order to come back to work, he was
again examined, but this time the physician examining him realized
that a mistake had been made in the original examination, as Kirkingburg
had a medical condition, amblyopia, that left him with 20/200 in the
left eye and essentially monocular vision.[77] Finally, since 1971, the
Department of Transportation (DOT) has required that a truck driver in
interstate commerce have corrected distant visual acuity and distant
binocular acuity of at least 20/40 in each eye.[78] Albertsons fired the

plaintiff because he could not meet DOT standards and refused to hire him once he had obtained a waiver from DOT (for a period of time, DOT had a program in effect where drivers demonstrating good performance could get a waiver of their vision requirements).[79]

Albertsons is notable for two points. First, how a person functions is not as important as the result of what the person does. That is, a person with a dominant eye that is normal may see perfectly well even though the other eye is deficient. This may be done by the brain itself or by an artificial aid. For example, I am dominant in either eye. When one eye gets tired, the other eye becomes dominant. It doesn't affect me in any way, as in my case glasses fully correct my vision in each eye. The only thing it forces me to do is occasionally adjust my rear view mirror when driving. Thus, so long as a person achieves the same result as the average person with respect to a major life activity, then that person is not limited in that major life activity.[80] Second, *Albertsons* is notable for affirming that the ADA does not trump other federal regulations.[81] Thus, Albertsons had a perfect right to insist on the vision requirements, as they were required by federal regulations, and should not have to suffer liability for enforcing those regulations that were properly formed according to administrative procedure.[82]

Justice Thomas filed a concurring opinion in *Albertsons.* His view was that one could rely on the DOT regulations as a defense to carry the day for Albertsons, but one could also argue that the plaintiff was not otherwise qualified to do the job.[83] That is, the plaintiff, due to the DOT regulation, was not able to meet the essential qualifications for the job due to his vision, and further, the ADA does not require an employer to eliminate an essential qualification for a particular job.[84]

A person who is only temporarily disabled does not have a disability under the ADA. In determining whether a person is "substantially limited in one or more of life's major activities," three factors need to be examined: the nature and severity of the disability, how long the disability will last or is expected to last, and the permanent or long-term impact or expected impact of the disability.[85] Thus, the ADA does not protect a person with a temporary disability.[86] So when does a temporary disability become permanent? If an employee has a disability that is likely to resolve itself over a period of a few months, should that person be accommodated? Since no clear answer exists for when a temporary disability becomes permanent, the decision to accommodate such a person becomes a philosophical question. Does the company act on the law or go beyond the law? Why would a company go beyond the law to do something it does not have to do? The concept of preventive law deals with this issue. One goal of preventive law is to stop problems before they occur.[87] Accommodating a person with a temporary disability prevents future problems from occurring because it enables that person to function at the same starting line as others for the duration of the impairment. It also prevents future litigation over whether the disability was, in fact, temporary and thus not covered under the provisions of the ADA. In addition, accommodating the person with a temporary disability increases the loyalty and productivity of that worker because he or she can continue to be part of the work force. Again, this is not to say that a company would not be within its rights to refuse to reasonably accommodate a temporary disability.

The second definition of disability under the ADA includes a person who has a record of an impairment regardless of whether he or she is currently substantially limited in a major life activity.[88] This definition commonly applies to people who have records of learning disabilities. Many students are diagnosed with learning disabilities very early in their education. Some outgrow those disabilities (some studies show that 80 percent of children with Attention Deficit Disorder outgrow it), and others learn to compensate for their learning disabilities without accommodations. Those persons will still be protected under the ADA and should not be discriminated against because of a documented learning disability.[89] The definition of discrimination is met if a record relied on by the employer indicates that the person either has or had a substantially limiting impairment.[90] The information could be found in medical records, education records, and personnel records, although with respect to personnel records, the ADA, due to a requirement that medical information not be contained in a person's personnel records, has lessened the likelihood of such information appearing there.

The final instance of a person having a disability under the ADA involves a person who is perceived as having an impairment.[91] This particular definition deals with attitudinal discrimination and can encompass three different circumstances:

1. A person has an impairment that is not substantially limiting but is perceived by the employer as substantially limiting;

2. A person has an impairment that is substantially limiting only because of the attitudes of others toward the impairment; or
3. A person has no impairment at all but is regarded by the employer as having a substantially limiting impairment.[92]

Often, people who discriminate jump to the wrong conclusion about whether a person has a disability. For example, an individual may assume that a gay person has HIV,[93] or a basketball referee association may assume that a person with glasses cannot referee a game because he or she does not see as well as a person without glasses or contacts. Also, while a more in-depth discussion of drug and alcohol abuse will follow later in this book, a person perceived as having a drug or alcohol problem is also protected under the ADA.[94]

Must a person, to be considered as being "regarded as" having a disability, be regarded as having both a physical or mental impairment *and* having a substantial limitation in a major life activity? The *Sutton* case answer this question. In the *Sutton* case, the plaintiffs argued in the alternative, that they were regarded as having a disability—in this case, the physical impairment of poor vision that substantially limited the major life activity of working.[95] Justice O'Connor, in writing for the Court, said that there were two possible ways a person could meet the third prong of the definition of a disability:

1. A covered entity—an employer, in this case—mistakenly believes that a person has a physical impairment that substantially limits one or more major life activities; or
2. A covered entity, again in this case an employer, mistakenly believes that an actual nonlimiting impairment substantially limits one or more major life activities.[96]

Note that in either case the *covered entity has to believe* that a major life activity is substantially limited.[97] In *Sutton,* very critically, the plaintiffs did not argue that they were regarded as being limited in the major life activity of seeing; rather, they argued that they were only limited in the major life activity of working.[98] That argument proved extremely damaging to the plaintiffs, because the Supreme Court held that if you argue that your client is limited in the major life activity of working, you have to show that the person is unable to perform a broad class of jobs.[99]

Thus, from *Sutton,* we now know that the "regarded as" prong means a person has to be regarded both as having a physical or mental impairment and as having an impairment that substantially limits one or more of life's major activities. We also know that it will continue to be extremely difficult for plaintiffs to prevail if they argue that the major life activity that is limited is the activity of working. I have long wondered why so many plaintiff lawyers over the years have argued that their client was limited in the major life activity of working, as many times another major life activity could just as easily be argued. Perhaps this decision will lead plaintiff lawyers away from arguing working as the major life activity. Of course, it is in the best interest of the defense lawyer to somehow get the case focused on working as the major life activity.

Finally, we come to the issue of *otherwise qualified.* A person may have a disability and not be protected under the ADA because he or she is not otherwise qualified. *Otherwise qualified* has two different meanings under the ADA, depending upon whether Title I (which applies to employers of fifteen or more employees) or Title II (which applies to governmental entities regardless of size) is at issue. Under Title I of the ADA, a person with a disabling condition is otherwise qualified if he or she satisfies the requisite skill, experience, and education requirements of the position and can, *with or without reasonable accommodation,* perform the essential functions of the job.[100] This definition, however, raises questions of its own, such as what is a reasonable accommodation (discussed in Chapter 3) and what is an essential function of a job (discussed in Chapter 2).

With respect to Title II of the ADA, a person is considered to be otherwise qualified if he or she can, *with or without reasonable modifications* to rules, policies, or practices; the removal of architectural, communication, or transportation barriers; or the provision of auxiliary aids and services, meet the essential eligibility requirements for receiving services or participating in programs or activities provided by a public entity.[101] Questions arise here as well. What is a reasonable modification in a program? How do you determine an essential eligibility requirement?

"Otherwise qualified" also arises in another context in ADA jurisprudence: that of direct threat. *Direct threat* is a term that was settled by the U.S. Supreme Court in *School Board of Nassau County, Florida v. Arline*. That case, involving a public school teacher terminated for having tuberculosis, held that whether a person is a direct threat (and to many courts' way of thinking, "not otherwise qualified") depends upon evaluating:

- the nature of the risk (how the disease is transmitted);
- the duration of the risk (how long the carrier is infectious);
- the severity of the risk (what the potential harm is to third parties); and
- the probabilities the disease will be transmitted and will cause varying degrees of harm.[102]

The regulations implementing Title I of the ADA (the Equal Employment Opportunity Commission is responsible for administering the regulations under Title I of the ADA) are very similar to the *Arline* standards. The EEOC regulations state that a person is a direct threat if:

- a significant risk of substantial harm exists;
- the specific risk is identifiable;
- the risk is a current risk—that is, not speculative or remote;
- the assessment of the risk is based upon objective medical or other factual evidence regarding the particular individual; and
- a genuine significant risk of substantial harm exists, and the employer cannot eliminate or remove the risk by reasonable accommodations.[103]

If a person is found to be a direct threat, many courts are finding that the person is not otherwise qualified and is therefore not protected under the ADA. This line of reasoning creates unnecessary confusion for someone trying to understand the workings of the ADA, even though the courts are committed to the terminology. I find it helps to think of "otherwise qualified" and "direct threat" as two different concepts,[104] both of which may result in a finding of not being otherwise qualified. Think of "otherwise qualified" as referring to whether a person can do the essential functions of the job with or without reasonable accommodations or a person effectively using a service with or without reasonable modifications. Thus, to follow this analysis through in the employment context, "direct threat" refers to when a person can do the essential functions of the job with or without reasonable accommodations, but that person performing the job would constitute a direct threat.[105]

Finally, is "direct threat" an affirmative defense or something that the plaintiff has to prove as part of his or her case? The answer depends on the Circuit. In the Eleventh Circuit, the case in point is *Moses v. American NonWovens Inc.*[106] In *Moses*, the plaintiff worked in several capacities for NonWovens, including as a product inspector, web operator, and hot splicer assistant.[107] All jobs involved working with exposed machinery, some of which became extremely hot.[108] Moses had epilepsy, and the employer fired Moses because the epilepsy posed a possible threat of an accident.[109] The issue before the court was whether it was up to the employer or up to Moses to show whether a direct threat existed. The court held that the employee, in this case Moses, had the burden to show that he was not a direct threat, and that he had not produced probative evidence that he was not a direct threat.[110]

The case of *EEOC v. Amego*, a First Circuit case, is slightly different.[111] *Amego* is interesting in several respects, not the least of which was that a provider of mental health and mental retardation services was sued by an employee for violation of the ADA.[112] In *Amego*, an employee who was responsible for overseeing a group home for persons with autism and other mental illnesses developed several serious problems: She became involved with a coworker who used cocaine; she suffered from clinical depression and eating disorders; and her attempts to treat her depression were unsuccessful.[113] As a result, her work performance suffered, and she attempted suicide twice by overdosing on medications.[114] Finally, there were indications that the medicine at the group home was not being monitored properly.[115] Amego eventually let the plaintiff go because they believed that she could not perform an essential function of the job—handling medications for persons in the group home—with or without reasonable accommodations and that she posed a risk to herself and others.[116] The district court found for Amego and the EEOC appealed.[117] The EEOC claimed, among other things, that direct threat is an affirmative defense, while Amego claimed that proving direct threat or the lack of it was part of the plaintiff's case.[118]

How did the court settle the issue? In a sense, the court split the difference. The court concluded that determining who has the burden of proof depends upon whether the essential job functions involve the safety of others. If the safety of others is involved in a job's essential functions, then it is up to the plaintiff to show that he or she is not a direct threat, and doing so would include showing that he or she is otherwise qualified.[119] However, if the safety of others is not involved in the job's essential functions, such as in the case involving the teacher with tuberculosis, then it is up to the employer to prove direct threat as an affirmative defense.[120] There is a third approach the Circuits take, and that is they consider "direct threat" to be an affirmative defense, and therefore, the burden is on the defense to make the showing of direct threat. This is the approach taken by the Seventh Circuit.[121] Thus, as is often the case with the ADA, we will have to follow further judicial developments to see how this particular question will play out.

With respect to "direct threat," the ADA itself does not mention whether "direct threat" applies to the person him- or herself or to other people.[122] The EEOC, in implementing the ADA's employment provisions, has said that "direct threat" applies where a person threatens his own health as well as the health of others.[123] In the case of *Chevron U.S.A. Inc. v. Echazabal*,[124] the U.S. Supreme Court was directly faced with this question. In *Chevron,* the plaintiff worked for independent contractors at an oil refinery owned by Chevron.[125] He applied for a job directly with Chevron twice and was offered the job if he could pass the company's physical.[126] Each time the plaintiff took the physical, the physical showed liver damage as a result of hepatitis C, which Chevron doctors said would be aggravated by his working at the oil refinery.[127] Each time the plaintiff applied, Chevron withdrew the offer.[128] The second time Chevron withdrew the offer, it asked that the plaintiff be reassigned to a job without exposure to harmful chemicals or be removed from the refinery altogether.[129] The plaintiff filed suit, claiming that this conduct violated the ADA.[130] Chevron relied on the direct threat defense as specified in the EEOC regulations.[131] In finding for Chevron, the U.S. Supreme Court relied upon an employer's obligations under the Occupational Safety and Health Act to provide a safe working environment for its employees.[132] The Court went on to note that the "direct threat" defense had to meet a fairly compelling standard.[133] More specifically, the Court said that the direct threat defense must be based upon a reasonable medical judgment relying on the most current medical knowledge and/or the best available objective evidence.[134] Further, this assessment must be based upon an individualized assessment of the individual's present ability to safely perform the essential functions of the job as described in the EEOC regulations.[135] Thus, it is now clear that "direct threat" applies to threats to an individual as well as threats to others.

All of this so far is beside the point if an employee is not involved. Just who is an employee under the ADA? The Supreme Court was faced with this very question in *Clackamas Gastroenterology Associates, P.C. v. Wells*.[136] In *Clackamas,* a bookkeeper brought an ADA discrimination claim against her employer, Clackamas Gastroenterology Associates.[137] Clackamas defended on the grounds that it did not have fifteen or more employees.[138] The question before the Court was whether the four physician shareholders who owned the corporation could be considered employees.[139] If the shareholders could be considered employees, then the statutory number of fifteen would be satisfied, but if they were not employees, then Clackamas did not have the requisite number of employees to be subject to the ADA.[140]

The Supreme Court held that whether a person is an employee comes down to just how much control is exercised over them.[141] For example, the Court looked to its prior case law to say that control can be measured by such things as: the skill required; the source of the instrumentalities and tools; the location of the work; the duration of the relationship between the parties; the hiring party's right to assign the work to another; the discretion the hiring party has over when and how long to work; the method of payment; the hiring party's role in hiring and paying assistants; the nature of the work insofar as it is a part of the regular business of the hiring party, etc.[142] For those familiar with Revenue Ruling 87-41,[143] which the Internal Revenue Service uses to decide whether a person is an independent contractor or an employee, that reader will most assuredly see the similarities. The Court went on to favorably cite EEOC guidelines on how one can determine whether a "partner" was in actuality an employee. Those guidelines lists six factors to use in making this determination: 1) whether the organization can hire or fire the individual or set the rules and regulations of the individual's work; 2) whether and, if so, to what extent the organization supervises the individual's work; 3) whether the individual reports to someone higher in the organization; 4) whether that individual is able to influence the organization; 5) whether the parties intended for the person to be an employee as specified in any written agreements or contracts; and 6) whether the individual shares in the profits or losses of the organization.[144] The Court noted that no one factor was dispositive; rather, the conclusion depends on "all incidents of the relationship."[145] Thus, the Court sent the matter back for further proceedings to see if the four physician shareholders were indeed employees.

So, how should the practitioner deal with the question of whether the person is an employee vis-á-vis the ADA and other federal antidiscrimination laws? A really good preventive approach that I have used in the past is Revenue Ruling 87-41, mentioned above. That revenue ruling is eerily similar to some of the Supreme Court case law, also noted above. The practitioner may also want to look at the EEOC guidance cited favorably by the Court in *Clackamas*.

NOTES

1. Equal Employment Opportunity Commission's Enforcement Guidance on Reasonable Accommodations, http://www.eeoc.gov/docs/accommodation.html at 9, no. 9 (1999).
2. 42 U.S.C. § 12102(2).
3. 29 C.F.R. § 1630.2(j).
4. Toyota Motor Mfg., Kentucky, Inc. v. Williams, 534 U.S. 184 (2002).
5. *Id.* at 187.
6. *Id.*
7. *Id.*
8. *Id.*
9. *Id.* at 188.
10. *Id.*
11. *Id.*
12. *Id.*
13. *Id.*
14. *Id.* at 189.
15. *Id.*
16. *Id.*
17. *Id.* at 189-90.
18. *Id.* at 190.
19. *Id.*
20. *Id.* at 195-96, *citing* 29 C.F.R. § 1630.2(j).
21. *Id.* at 196.
22. *Id.* at 196-98.
23. EEOC v. Sears Roebuck & Co., 417 F.3d 789 (7th Cir. 2005), 2005 U.S. App. LEXIS 16707.
24. *Id.* at 2005 U.S. App. LEXIS 16707, *2-5.
25. *Id.* at *4.
26. *Id.*
27. *Id.* at *7.
28. *Id.*

29. *Id.* at *2.
30. *Id.*
31. *Id.*
32. *Id.* at *2-3.
33. *Id.* at *11.
34. *Id.* at *19-20.
35. *See id.* at *33-51.
36. *Id.* at *23.
37. *Id.* at *24.
38. *Id.* at *27.
39. *Id.* at *30.
40. *Id.*
41. *See id.* at *31; *but see* Scheerer v. Potter, _ F.3d_, 2006 U.S. App. LEXIS 868 (7th Cir. April 10, 2006) (extending Toyota Motor's definition of "substantially limits" to a person with diabetes).
42. *See* 29 C.F.R. § 1630.2(j).
43. *Toyota Motor,* 534 U.S. at p. 198.
44. Sutton v. United Air Lines, 527 U.S. 471 (1999).
45. *Id.*
46. *Id.* at 475.
47. *Id.* at 476.
48. *Id.* at 475.
49. *Id.* at 481.
50. *Id.* at 481-82.
51. *Id.* at 482.
52. *Id.*
53. *Id.* There is an unfortunate implication here with this statement, and it is one often seen in ADA decisions. That is, there seems to be an assumption that mitigating measures cure a disability. While that is often true with glasses, it is hardly ever true for any other disability. For example, a person with my hearing loss will never have a normal hearing loss with hearing aids. What hearing aids will do is bring that person as close as possible to the normal hearing loss range given his or her loss; in my case the number would be 40%. After that, it is up to the individual to use other ways to compensate so as to be able to function in the hearing world. I do that by being an expert lip reader with a comprehensive understanding of the English language. In that way, I am able to function as if I were a normal hearing person, though in truth I am not.
54. *Id.*
55. *Id.* at 483.
56. *Id.* at 484.
57. *Id.* at 485-87; *see also id.* at 494-95 (Ginsburg, J., concurring).
58. *Id.* at 490-91.
59. *Id.* at 495 (Stevens, J., dissenting).
60. *Id.* at 495-96.

61. *Id.* at 498.
62. *Id.* at 509-10.
63. *Id.* at 499-501.
64. *Id.* at 505.
65. *Id.* at 506-07.
66. *See id.* at 499-500.
67. *Id.* at 503.
68. *Id.* at 513 (Breyer, J., dissenting).
69. *See Scheerer, supra.*
70. It is a myth that hearing aids can help all persons with hearing loss, as all hearing aids do is amplify sounds; they do nothing to improve a person's ability to comprehend those sounds.
71. To decide which standard the medical expert will testify to, the reader will have to research whether his or her jurisdiction follows *Sears, Roebuck & Co., supra* (holding that *Toyota Motor's* definition of "substantially limits" was limited to performing manual tasks), or *Scheerer, supra,* and other cases like it (holding that *Toyota Motor's* definition of "substantially limits" extends across all major life activities).
72. Albertsons v. Kirkingburg, 527 U.S. 555 (1999).
73. *Id.* at 558.
74. *Id.*
75. *Id.* at 559.
76. *Id.*
77. *Id.*
78. *Id.* at 558-59.
79. *Id.* at 560.
80. *Id.* at 565-66.
81. *Id.* at 570. In addition to page 570, the reader is referred to footnote 16 on that page where the court says that the regulations implementing Title I of the ADA explicitly allow compliance with federal law or regulations as a defense to liability. The majority opinion, though implicitly recognizing this in an approving manner in the pages that follow, says that they do not consider the effect of such regulations, since the parties never brought it up. However, Justice Thomas would have based the decision itself on the defense allowed by the regulations. *See id.* at 578 (Thomas, J., concurring).
82. *Id.* at 573-77 (Opinion for the Court).
83. Id. at 578 (Thomas, J., concurring).
84. *Id.* at 579-80.
85. 29 C.F.R. § 1630.2(j)(2). The DOJ regulations on Titles II and III of the ADA contain identical wording.
86. Burch v. Coca Cola Co., 119 F.3d 305, 316 (1997).
87. William D. Goren. *An Ideal Fit: The ADA and Preventive Law,* 14 PREVENTIVE L. REP. 19 (1995).

88. 42 U.S.C. § 12102(2)(B).
89. *See* comments to 29 C.F.R. § 1630.2(k).
90. *Id.*
91. 42 U.S.C. § 12102(2)(c).
92. *Id.* at 322.
93. *See* 29 C.F.R. § 1630.2(l) and Interpretive Guidance regarding same.
94. *See* Miners v. Cargill Commc'ns, Inc., 133 F.3d 820 (8th Cir. 1997). This case is discussed in depth later in this book.
95. *Sutton*, 527 U.S. at 490.
96. *Id.* at 489.
97. *Id.*
98. *Id.* at 490-92.
99. *Id.* at 491.
100. 29 C.F.R. § 1630.2(m).
101. 28 C.F.R. § 35.104.
102. School Board of Nassau County, Fla. v. Arline, 480 U.S. 273, 288, 94 L. Ed. 2d 307, 107 Sup. Ct. 1123 (1987).
103. 29 C.F.R. § 1630.2(r).
104. *See* EEOC v. Amego, Inc., 110 F.3d 135, 142 (1st Cir. 1997).
105. *Id.* at 142-43.
106. Moses v. Am. Nonwovens, Inc., 97 F.3d 446 (11th Cir. 1996).
107. *Id.* at 447-48.
108. *Id.*
109. *Id.* at 447.
110. *Id.*
111. EEOC v. Amego, Inc., 110 F.3d 135 (1st Cir. 1997).
112. *Id.* at 137.
113. *Id.* at 138-39.
114. *Id.* at 139.
115. *Id.*
116. *Id.* at 141.
117. *Id.*
118. *Id.* at 141-42.
119. *Id.* at 144.
120. *Id.*
121. Branham v. Snow, 392 F.3d 896, 906-07 & n.5.
122. *See* 42 U.S.C.S. § 12111(3) (2005).
123. *See* 29 C.F.R. § 1630.2(r)(2005).
124. Chevron v. Echazabal, 536 U.S. 73 (2002).
125. *Id.* at 76.
126. *Id.*
127. *Id.*
128. *Id.*
129. *Id.*
130. *Id.*

131. *Id.*

132. *Id.* at 84-85.

133. *Id.* at 85-86.

134. *Id.* at 86.

135. *Id.*

136. Clackamas Gastroenterology Assocs., P.C. v. Wells, 538 U.S. 440 (2003).

137. *Id.* at 442.

138. *Id.*

139. *Id.*

140. *Id.*

141. *Id.* at 448.

142. *Id.* at 445 n.5.

143. Rev. Rul. 87-41, 1987-1 C.B. 296.

144. *Clackamas,* 538 U.S. at 448.

145. *Id.* at 449 n.8.

Essential Functions of the Job $\quad$ **2**

IN THE DEFINITION of "otherwise qualified" in the employment context, the term *essential function* plays a critical role. How do you determine the essential functions of a job? The EEOC has said it will look at the following factors:

- The employer's judgment
- A written job description prepared before advertising or interviewing applicants for a job
- The amount of time spent performing the function
- The consequences of not requiring a person in the particular job to perform a function
- Work experience of people who have performed a job in the past and of people who currently perform similar jobs
- The nature of the work operation and the organizational structure of the employer

These factors can become complicated when they are applied to a particular case. However, determining essential functions does not have to be complicated. Think of essential functions as any element of the job fundamental to achieving the job's purpose. Those elements that are not fundamental can be classified as marginal functions. For example, consider the job of the lawyer. In order to be a lawyer, one must be able to research legal matters and communicate the findings. Does the person have to be able to appear in court? Most lawyers never see the inside of a courtroom, and so appearing in court for those lawyers would not be considered fundamental to their job.

The example above raises another issue: The essential functions of a job need to be accurate. If typing sixty words a minute is required by the job but the person in that position never typed more than forty words a minute, then sixty words a minute is not an essential function of the job—forty words a minute is.[2]

Finally, two mistakes are frequently made when assessing essential functions of a job. First, essential functions are often confused with major life activities—an entirely different concept. For instance, hearing is not an essential function of being a lawyer. An essential function of being a lawyer is being able to gather and process information and to communicate it to others. Whether the person hears or communicates in sign language doesn't matter. Similarly, hearing is not an essential function of the job of being a softball umpire. Calling balls and strikes and outs quickly and accurately are among the essential functions of that job.

What about sight? Is seeing an essential function of refereeing? Perhaps surprisingly, the answer is no; calling the game accurately is. Of course, without sight the game cannot be called accurately; therefore, the person would not be protected under the ADA, because he or she could not do the essential functions of the job with or without reasonable accommodations. Even so, a major life activity and an essential function are not the same. Thus, the person who can't see and wants to umpire a game does not have a valid ADA claim, not because he can't see (the life activity) but because he can't perform the essential functions of the job—making accurate calls, with or without reasonable accommodations.

The second problem area is confusing essential functions of the job with tasks. For example, is ten-key data entry an essential function of a data entry job? The answer is no; ten-key data entry is a task, not a function. The essential function of the job is data entry at a certain rate of speed; how it gets done doesn't matter. The only exception would be if it could be shown that data entry for the particular job could only be done through ten-key.

Finally, in determining essential functions, it is helpful if the particular job has been analyzed to determine the components. That can be accomplished by hiring consultants and talking to the person who does the job. It also means keeping job descriptions current. Most jobs are dynamic, and their essential functions change over time. Thus, if a job description is not current, the employee may have the opportunity later to allege that her or his essential job functions were different from those contained in the job description. Also, keeping the lines of communication open between employees and employer should help ensure that the essential functions of a job are monitored properly.

In short, determining essential functions of the job does not have to be complicated. If it is handled correctly, the employer benefits by avoiding costly litigation and plaintiff verdicts. The employee benefits by receiving more freedom to accomplish his or her job in accordance with his or her capabilities.

If a case is in trial, who determines essential functions of the job—the judge or the jury? A case that addressed this question is *Barber v. Nabors Drilling U.S.A., Inc.*[3] In *Barber*, Nabors refused to allow the plaintiff to return to his job as a tool pusher on an oil-drilling rig after he received treatment for a back injury.[4] The plaintiff throughout the course of the litigation maintained that he was capable of performing the essential functions of the job.[5] In determining that the jury should decide a job's essential functions, the Fifth Circuit stated:

> If we venture to second-guess then we simply usurp the most critical function of the jury in ADA cases, i.e., the injection of some indispensable common sense in the determination of what is or is not an essential function. When a statutory scheme such as the ADA necessitates some seemingly arbitrary line-drawing exercise, courts of law do well to refer the question to the jury, and consequently the appellate court must respect the jury's call, unless it is unsupportable by the evidence.[6]

Finally, the court said:

> A highly deferential standard is especially appropriate with regard to the jury's determination of what the essential functions

of the job are, since the evidence, as in this case, most often consists of *post hoc* descriptions of what the employee was expected to do and what he actually did, which necessarily requires the jury to judge the credibility of witnesses and the veracity of their testimony.[7]

Thus, an argument can be made that essential functions of the job are a question of fact for the jury to decide and not a question of law to be decided on summary judgment.

NOTES

1. 29 C.F.R. § 1630.2(n).
2. *See* EEOC's Interpretive Guidance to 29 C.F.R. § 1630.2(n).
3. Barber v. Nabors Drilling U.S.A., Inc., 130 F.3d 702 (5th Cir. 1997).
4. *Id.* at 704.
5. *Id.*
6. *Id.* at 708.
7. *Id.*

Concept of Undue Hardship and Reasonable Accommodation in the Employment Context

3

What is a reasonable accommodation in the employment context? Under the ADA, reasonable accommodation is defined in the negative. More specifically, a reasonable accommodation is anything that does not constitute an undue hardship.[1] Thus, it becomes imperative to know what an undue hardship is. In determining whether an accommodation is an undue hardship, the EEOC will look to several factors:

- The nature and net cost of the accommodation needed. Keep in mind that any reimbursements, tax deductions, and the like are counted against the employer.
- The overall financial resources of the facility or facilities, the number of persons employed at the facility, and the effect of the reasonable accommodation on expenses and resources.
- The overall financial resources of the covered entity, the overall size of the business of the covered entity with respect to the number of its em-

ployees, and the number, type, and location of its facilities.

■ The type of operation or operations of the covered entity, including the composition, structure, and functions of the work force of such entity, and the geographic separateness and administrative or fiscal relationship of the facility or facilities in question to the covered entity.

■ The impact of the accommodation on the operation of the facility, including the impact on the ability of other employees to perform their duties and on the facility's ability to conduct business.[2]

Other critical points about undue hardship must also be considered. First, the EEOC believes, which may or may not be the view of the U.S. Supreme Court, that undue hardship is measured against the entire operations of the employer and not just one department.[3] Thus, for example, Person X works in the MIS department. Person X has a disability, and everybody agrees that he needs an accommodation that will cost $600. The MIS department is just one division of a multimillion-dollar company. Whether the accommodation will constitute an undue hardship is, in the EEOC's view, measured against the entire operations of the company and not just the MIS division. Second, a business does not have to make an accommodation when that accommodation will fundamentally alter the nature of its business.[4] Thus, the employer generally is going to be better off arguing that the accommodation needed will fundamentally alter its operations rather than argue undue hardship. This is especially true because the data consistently show that fully 88 percent of all accommodations cost less than $1,000.

Finally, it bears noting that undue hardship does not equal inconvenience. Undue hardship is a term of art, and unless the accommodation rises to the level of a fundamental alteration in the business or is an undue hardship under the factors listed above, it is irrelevant if the accommodation inconveniences the employer. It is amazing how often one hears that businesses do not have to reasonably accommodate because doing so is not convenient. It also bears noting that the ADA applies to all activities, programs, and benefits of an organization. Thus, the rules of reasonable accommodation apply to preemployment skills testing as well, and any preemployment skills testing must be designed to measure the person's abilities and not his or her disabilities.[5]

What steps can an employer take to deal with the issue of reasonable accommodation? First, keep the lines of communication open between the employer and the employee. Open communication is critical to prevent problems from occurring due to a *misperception* of reasonable accommodation: that is, that the employee's requests must be honored at the risk of violating the ADA. That is simply not true. Deciding on implementing a reasonable accommodation is a process subject to negotiation between the employer and the employee. The key is to determine a way to get the employee with a disability to the same starting line as the person without a disability. The employer, through the negotiation process, has the flexibility to determine how.[6]

Second, be creative. What can be a reasonable accommodation is limited only by the parties' imagination. The employee will often know what accommodation is needed to do the essential functions of the job. It's not unusual for a company to estimate the cost of an accommodation and proceed through the approval process (often meeting resistance), only to be told by the employee, "All I need is this," at a cost far less than originally contemplated by the company.

Third, remember that no two disabilities are precisely the same, and every case must be analyzed on its own merits. For example, just because a person with one disability needs certain accommodations does not mean that a different person with the same disability needs the same accommodations.[7]

Fourth, the concept of good faith bears discussing. An employer who exercises good faith in dealing with a reasonable accommodation request is protected from damages stemming from intentional discrimination.[8] Some preventive steps to help ensure that a defendant can be found to have acted in good faith might include the following:

- Demonstrate a willingness to try multiple accommodations for the person's disability.
- Document any and all attempts at reasonable accommodations.
- Keep the lines of communication open.
- Have the accommodation process be cooperative rather than adversarial in nature.
- Demonstrate a record of creativity in dealing with the accommodation request.

Preventive steps are critical because an employer can be held liable for refusing to engage in the interactive process. To explain, it is helpful to return to the case of *EEOC v. Sears*, discussed above. The facts of this case are mentioned earlier in this book; however, more facts are needed at this point. Particular facts that bear noting here include: 1) Keane asked her immediate supervisor if she could eat lunch in the intimate apparel stock room so as to minimize her walking on the job.[9] Initially, her request was granted, but subsequently the supervisor announced a blanket policy preventing all eating in the stockroom.[10] 2) As Keane's condition worsened, she asked her immediate supervisor if she could walk through the shoe stockroom when going between the employee swipe-in area and the intimate apparel department.[11] She was referred to the manager of the shoe department, who denied her request.[12] Keane's immediate supervisor then went to the store manager, David Allen, who also denied her request.[13] 3) At some point, her immediate supervisor gave Keane permission to use the shoe stockroom as a shortcut; however, the first day she attempted to use the shortcut, a superior yelled at her to get out of there and also stated that the person who gave her permission had no business doing so.[14] Subsequently, the store manager posted someone at the entrance to the shoe stockroom and drafted a person to bar anyone from going through the door.[15] 4) Keane also asked the store manager if she could park near the merchandise pickup lot by the employee entrance.[16] The store manager denied the request and suggested that Keane use the parking space reserved for persons with disabilities.[17] However, parking in the persons with disabilities space meant that Keane still had to walk across the store to the employee swipe-in location and then walk back to her work area at the beginning and end of each shift.[18] 5) Eventually, the store manager asked Keane to have a doctor fill out a Sears physician certification form (Sears already had in its possession one doctor's note).[19] Keane's general practitioner completed the form and noted the diagnosis.[20] He recommended that Keane limit excessive walking and be allowed easy short access to her job site.[21] However, when the store manager received the form, he assumed that the reserved parking space near her department was sufficient to accommodate Keane and informed her immediate supervisor that Keane would not be allowed to cut through the shoe stockroom.[22] The store manager never asked for any additional information.[23]

In finding that Sears could be held liable for failure to accommodate Keane, the Seventh Circuit reasoned as follows. First, the Seventh Circuit set forth what is needed to prove a plaintiff's claim of the failure of an employer to accommodate a person with a disability. In order to prove a claim of disability discrimination based on an employer's failure to reasonably accommodate a person with a disability, a plaintiff has to show that: 1) she is a qualified individual with a disability; 2) the employer was aware of the plaintiff's disability; and 3) the employer failed to reasonably accommodate the plaintiff's disability.[24] Earlier in this book, we addressed whether Keane had a disability. We now turn to whether she was able to show that Sears was aware of her disability and that Sears failed to reasonably accommodate it. First, the Seventh Circuit said that the ADA imposes on the employee the obligation to initially inform the employer of a disability.[25] Second, where the notice of a disability to the employer from the employee is ambiguous, but is sufficient to notify the employer that the employee may have a disability requiring accommodation, the employer has the obligation to ask the employee for clarification.[26] Thus, an employer is not allowed "to shield itself from liability by choosing not to follow up on an employee's request for assistance or by intentionally remaining in the dark."[27] Third, the court noted that Keane gave to Sears two different doctors' notes of her diagnosis and the recommendation that she be permitted to avoid walking long distances.[28] Finally, the court noted that Keane, all told, had informed three different levels of Sears management of her disability.[29]

The Seventh Circuit having found that the plaintiff had a disability and that her employer was aware of the disability, now turned its attention to whether Sears failed to accommodate that disability. The court held that Sears could be liable for failing to accommodate the plaintiff's disability for the following reasons. First, once an employee discloses the disability to the employer, the employer is obligated under the ADA to engage the employee in an interactive process to determine the appropriate accommodation under the circumstances.[30] Second, the employer then has the obligation to engage in a give-and-take process with the employee with a disability so that both parties can determine what accommodation will enable the employee to continue working.[31] If this process does not lead to reasonable accommodation of the person with a disability, the responsibility for the failure to reasonably accommodate the employee lies with the party that causes the breakdown.[32] Third, an employer will not be liable for failure to accommodate where the employer acts in good faith during the interactive process and the employee refuses to participate or withholds essential information.[33] Fourth, if an employee requests an appropriate accommodation, the employer cannot simply reject that request without offering other suggestions or at least expressing the willingness to continue discussing possible accommodations through the interactive process.[34] That is, an employer cannot simply reject an employee's request for an accommodation without explaining why that request has been rejected or offering alternatives.[35] Finally, the court concluded that the plaintiff had made several specific requests for accommodation; however, Sears did not engage in the interactive process, and in fact, Sears disengaged itself from the interactive process altogether.[36] Accordingly, the Seventh Circuit reversed the lower court's award of summary judgment for Sears.[37]

With respect to reasonable accommodations, another question arises of whether a person regarded by the employer as having a disability is entitled to a reasonable accommodation. On this, the various circuits in the U.S. Court of Appeals are split. Circuits holding that reasonable accommodations are not available in such a case include the Ninth Circuit, the Eighth Circuit, the Sixth Circuit, and the Fifth Circuit.[38] Circuits holding that reasonable accommodations are available in such a case include the Third Circuit, the First Circuit, the Tenth Circuit,[39] and the Eleventh Circuit.[40] Why a court might hold that reasonable accommodations are available for an employee where the employer perceives a person as having a disability can be explained by reviewing the decision of the 10th Circuit in *Kelly v. Metallics West Inc.*[41] The facts of *Kelly* are as follows. Kelly started working for Metallics West in April 1996 as a receptionist.[42] In August of 1999, she was promoted to customer service supervisor.[43] A critical function of the customer service supervisor was inputting incoming orders.[44] In mid-May 2000, she was hospitalized due to a blood clot or pulmonary embolism in her lung.[45] She was discharged from the hospital on May 22 and returned home on supplemental oxygen.[46] On May 30, Kelly's physician cleared her to return to work without supplemental oxygen.[47] Returning to work without oxygen did not work for Kelly.[48] On June 1, Kelly went back to her doctor, who wrote her a note stating that she needed to use oxygen at work.[49] When Kelly went through Metallics West to clear the use of oxygen at work, Metallics West informed her that they would not allow that and that she should file for short-term disability instead.[50] Kelly went on short-term disability and once the embolism had resolved, the doctor released her to return to work without oxygen.[51] When she did return to work sometime after being released by her doctor, the attempt again did not go well.[52] Therefore, the doctor released her to return to work with oxygen.[53] Once again, Metallics West would not allow oxygen on the premises.[54] They stated that they were worried that she might "fall over dead."[55] That conversation led to a management meeting at which it was decided that Kelly would be terminated.[56] Finally, there was no dispute that Kelly was capable of performing the essential functions of the job as long as she had her oxygen.[57] After Metallics West motioned for summary judgment on the grounds that Kelly's impairment was temporary and, in any event, could be alleviated by portable oxygen, the district court permitted the claim to proceed anyway on the theory that Metallics West perceived Kelly as disabled and terminated her as a result of that perception.[58]

In concluding that reasonable accommodations were available to a person regarded as disabled, the Tenth Circuit concluded as follows. First, the court looked to the definition of a disability under the Americans with Disabilities Act. The court began by noting that the Americans with Disabilities Act prohibits discrimination against a qualified individual with a disability.[59] Further, they noted that under the Americans with Disabilities Act, a qualified individual is defined as an individual with a disability who, with or without reasonable accommodations, can perform the essential functions of the employment position.[60] The court also noted that a disability under the Americans with Disabilities Act includes a person who is regarded as having an impairment that substantially limits one or more life's major activities.[61] From this, the Tenth Circuit reasoned that the ADA protects an individual regarded as disabled but who with reasonable accommodations can perform the essential functions of the job.[62]

Second, the court disagreed with other courts that said to allow such accommodations would result in people regarded as having a disability having advantages over those not having disabilities when in fact neither had a disability under the ADA.[63] The court said this argument makes little sense because the person seeking protection is doing so not because of an impairment but because of being regarded as having a disability.[64]

Third, the court said the argument that to hold that a person regarded as having a disability did not have to be accommodated would lead to employees doing nothing to educate employers of their capabilities or to encourage the employer to see their employees' talents clearly made no sense.[65] In the court's view, an employer unable or unwilling to shed its stereotypical assumptions based on faulty or prejudiced perceptions of the employee's abilities has to be prepared to accommodate the artificial limitations created by the employer's own faulty perceptions.[66] Such a view encourages employers to become more enlightened about employees' capabilities while protecting employees from employers whose attitudes remain steeped in prejudice.[67]

Finally, the court said that Congress, in writing the Americans with Disabilities Act, apparently believed it was reasonable to ask employers to reasonably accommodate people regarded as having a disability because the Americans with Disabilities Act makes no distinction between employees who are actually disabled and those who are merely regarded as disabled when it comes to the definition of reasonable accommodation.[68]

Ultimately, the U.S. Supreme Court will have to decide this question as the Circuits are split. Being a student of ADA decisions issuing from the U.S. Supreme Court for years now, I have completely given up trying to predict how the Court might decide an individual ADA case. This is especially true now with the advent of Chief Justice Roberts and Justice Alito to the U.S. Supreme Court.

NOTES

1. 42 U.S.C. § 12112(b)(5)(A).
2. 29 C.F.R. § 1630.2(p)(2).
3. 29 C.F.R. § 1630.2(p)(2)(ii), (iii), *but see* Olmstead v. L.C. by Zimring, 527 U.S. 581, 597 (1999), majority opinion of J. Ginsburg, holding in a Title II case that looking to the entire resources of a public entity to determine undue burden/fundamental alteration may not be appropriate.
4. 29 C.F.R. § 1630.15(d).
5. *See* 29 C.F.R. § 1630.2(o)(3) and Interpretive Guidance regarding same.
6. *See, e.g.,* Johnson v. Lancaster-Lebanon, 757 F. Supp. 606, 617 (E.D. Pa., 1991) (a case arising under IDEA).
7. 42 U.S.C. § 1981a(a)(3).
8. *Sears Roebuck & Co.*, 2005 U.S. App. LEXIS 16707, *3.
9. *Id.* at *4.
10. *Id.*
11. *Id.*
12. *Id.*
13. *Id.* at *5-6.
14. *Id.* at *6.
15. *Id.*
16. *Id.*
17. *Id.*

18. *Id.* at *7.
19. *Id.*
20. *Id.*
21. *Id.*
22. *Id.*
23. *Id.* at *16.
24. *Id.* at *37.
25. *Id.* at *38.
26. *Id.*
27. *Id.* at *39.
28. *Id.*
29. *Id.* at *41-43.
30. *Id.* at *43.
31. *Id.*
32. *Id.* at *44.
33. *Id.* at *46-47.
34. *Id.* at *47.
35. *Id.*at *48-50.
36. *Id.* at *51.
37. *See* Kelly v. Metallics West, Inc., 410 F.3d 670, 675 (10th Cir. 2005) and the cases cited therein.
38. *Id.*
39. D'Angelo v. Conagra Foods, Inc., 2005 U.S. App. LEXIS 18639 (11th Cir. Aug. 30, 2005).
40. Kelly v. Metallics West, Inc., 410 F.3d 670 (10th Cir. 2005).
41. *Id.* at 671.
42. *Id.* at 671-72.
43. *Id.* at 672.
44. *Id.*
45. *Id.*
46. *Id.*
47. *Id.*
48. *Id.*
49. *Id.*
50. *Id.*
51. *Id.*
52. *Id.*
53. *Id.*
54. *Id.*
55. *Id.* at 673.
56. *Id.* at 672.
57. *Id.* at 673.
58. *Id.* at 675.
59. *Id.*
60. *Id.*

61. *Id.*
62. *Id.* at 676.
63. *Id.*
64. *Id.*
65. *Id.*
66. *Id.*
67. *Id.*
68. *Id.*

Treatment of Alcoholics and Drug Addicts 4

THE TREATMENT OF ALCOHOLICS and drug addicts needs to be discussed separately, as they are governed by an entirely different set of rules. The ADA makes a distinction between recovering from drug abuse and actively using drugs.[1] Using drugs is not protected under the ADA. However, a person who has a record of drug use that substantially limits one or more of life's major activities is disabled for the purposes of the ADA.[2] Casual drug use in the past is not indicative of a disability, while substantial use is.[3] Determining whether the usage in the past was casual or substantial is not always easy. A person in a rehabilitation program or a person who has completed a rehabilitation program is disabled for purposes of the ADA.[4]

Furthermore, if an employer makes an erroneous assumption that a person is using drugs or alcohol, the person is considered disabled because he or she is *perceived* as having a mental or physical impairment that substantially limits one or more of life's major activities.[5] The risk to an employer that erroneously perceives a disability, or perceives a disability without proof, is very real, as the case of *Miners v. Cargill Communications, Inc.* makes clear.[6] In *Miners*, the plaintiff worked as a promotions director for a radio station, where part of her job involved going to bars to promote the radio station in a company van.[7] After a while, her supervisor, a recovering alcoholic, became suspicious that the plaintiff was drinking while at the bars.[8] A private investigator hired to follow the plaintiff observed her drinking and then called the supervisor.[9] The supervisor showed up at the bar and, when the plaintiff left, demanded the keys to the company van.[10]

The next day the president of the radio station informed the plaintiff that she faced termination unless she entered a chemical dependency program.[11] The plaintiff declined to enter the program and was terminated.[12] She brought suit alleging that she was terminated on the basis of a perceived disability—alcoholism—and not because she violated a company rule.[13] The court found that sufficient evidence existed that the plaintiff had been fired because of a perceived disability.[14]

In addition to the need for clear company policy, the lesson here is that the employer needs to examine all options before acting on a disability. It is entirely possible that the plaintiff was indeed an alcoholic. However, just observing the plaintiff drinking in a bar does not make her one. The employer would have been better off requesting a medical exam on the grounds that it was job-related and a business necessity (to be discussed in the next chapter). The exam could help determine how to proceed, and, if necessary, justify the termination of the plaintiff. Alternatively, the employer could have focused on conduct and used a "no drinking" policy as the basis of some disciplinary action.

A person with an alcohol problem could well have a disability under the ADA, as the *Miners* case makes clear. Also, a person who has been in alcohol rehabilitation is protected under the ADA. However, unlike with mental and physical disabilities, an employer can evaluate the alcoholic employee as if the disability didn't exist.[15] This is a critical distinction between alcohol and other disabilities. For example, if an alcoholic's job performance declines, the alcoholic can be evaluated based on that performance. On the other hand, it would be a violation of the ADA to deny a person with a mental or physical disability a reasonable accommodation and then evaluate their performance without the accommodation.

NOTES

1. 29 C.F.R. § 1630.3 and Interpretive Guidance regarding same.
2. 29 C.F.R. § 1630.3(b)(1), (2).
3. Hartman v. City of Petaluma, 841 F. Supp. 946, 949 (N.D. Cal. 1994).
4. 29 C.F.R. § 1630.3(b)(1).
5. 29 C.F.R. § 1630.3(b)(3).
6. Miners v. Cargill Commc'ns, Inc., 113 F.3d 820 (8th Cir. 1997).
7. *Id.* at 821.
8. *Id.* at 821-22.
9. *Id.* at 822.
10. *Id.*
11. *Id.*
12. *Id.*
13. *Id.*
14. *Id.* at 824.
15. EEOC Interpretive Guidance on 29 C.F.R. § 1630.16(b).

Preemployment Medical Exams/Disability-Related Inquiries

5

WITH RESPECT TO PREEMPLOYMENT medical *exams*, a different issue from preemployment medical *inquiries*, the EEOC has issued guidelines on this as well.[1] The EEOC defines a prohibited medical exam as any tests or procedures seeking information about an individual's physical or mental impairment or physical or psychological health.[2] In assessing whether a test is a prohibited preemployment medical exam, the EEOC will look to the following eight factors:

1. Whether the test is administered by a health-care professional or trainee;
2. Whether the results of the test are interpreted by a health-care provider or trainee;
3. Whether the test is designed to reveal an impairment or the state of an individual's physical or psychological health;
4. Whether the employer is administering the procedure or test for the purpose of revealing the existence, nature or severity of an impairment, or the subject's general physical or psychological health;
5. Whether the test is invasive;

6. Whether the test measures physiological or psychological responses as opposed to performance of tasks;
7. Whether the test is normally done in a medical setting; and
8. Whether medical equipment or devices are used for the test.[3]

Two critical points: First, one or more of the above factors may be enough for the EEOC to determine that a prohibited preemployment medical exam is involved.[4] Second, even if a preemployment medical exam is not involved, there still could be a preemployment disability-related inquiry within that exam, and that inquiry would be in violation of the ADA.[5]

The issue of preemployment disability-related inquiries within the context of nonmedical exams will arise frequently in the area of psychological preemployment testing. Employers use such tests for many reasons, and such tests are not considered medical exams because they generally do not meet the EEOC criteria mentioned above. Nevertheless, most of these tests will contain preemployment disability-related inquiries, and thus portions of the test will violate the ADA. Unfortunately, when the ADA-violative portions of the tests are removed, it is conceivable, if not likely, that the validity of the whole test would be compromised. In short, expect to see more litigation in the area of preemployment psychological testing. Employers would do well to have such tests reviewed to see if they are in fact medical exams issued preemployment or if they contain impermissible preemployment disability-related inquiries. An employer that fails to have these tests reviewed may wind up suffering the same fate as the defendant in *Karraker v. Rent-A-Center, Inc.*[6] In *Karraker*, brothers desired to be promoted at the company they worked for, Rent-A-Center, Inc. The company required employees seeking promotion to take the ATP management training executive profile.[7] This battery of nine tests was designed to measure math and language skills as well as interests and personality traits,[8] and included 502 questions from the Minnesota Multiphasic Personality Inventory tests (MMPI).[9] The defendant said it used the MMPI to measure personality traits.[10] However, as the court noted, the MMPI considers where an applicant falls on scales measuring traits such as depression, hypochondriasis, hysteria, paranoia, and mania.[11] Further, the court noted that elevated scores on certain scales of the MMPI are used in the diagnosis of certain psychiatric disorders.[12] The way the defendant scored the battery of tests taken for promotion, it was possible for a person to be denied promotion based solely on his MMPI score.[13] The Karrakers, who were denied a promotion based on their MMPI results, sued on behalf of themselves and other employees of the 106 Illinois Rent-A-Center stores, claiming that using the MMPI as a basis for promotion violated the Americans with Disabilities Act.[14] The district court held that the MMPI did not violate the ADA, and the Karrakers appealed.[15]

The Seventh Circuit, in holding for the plaintiffs, reasoned as follows. First, the court noted that people with psychiatric disabilities frequently faced attitudinal barriers resulting from unfounded stereotypes and prejudice.[16] Second, the court referred to the EEOC definition of a medical examination as a procedure or test seeking information about an individual's physical or mental impairment or health.[17] The court referred to the EEOC's test, mentioned above, and which appears in the EEOC's Enforcement Guidance on Preemployment Disability-Related Questions and Medical Examinations,[18] for determining whether a medical examination occurred.[19]

The court went on to note that one of these factors may be enough to determine that a medical examination is involved.[20] The defendant offered various explanations as to why the MMPI was used as a means of promoting its employees, but the Seventh Circuit was not persuaded.[21] The court said that either the MMPI was a very poor predictor of an applicant's potential as a manager (and posited that this might be the reason the MMPI was no longer used by the defendant as a means of testing employees seeking promotions), or the tests were designed to measure more than just an applicant's mood on a given day.[22] The court went on to note that the EEOC gives three examples of psychological tests that might or might not be considered medical exams.[23] The court noted that the first example given by the EEOC— where an employer uses a psychological test to assess tastes and habits—bears a close resemblance to the test used in this case.[24] In that example, the EEOC notes that while the employer may be presumably testing for one thing, the same test is routinely used in a clinical setting to provide evidence leading to a diagnosis of a mental disorder or impairment.[25] The court concluded that the defendant's use of the MMPI was being used in the same way by the defendant as it was being used by the hypothetical defendant in the aforementioned EEOC example.[26] Thus, the Seventh Circuit held that the battery of tests used by the defendant were a medical exam having the likely effect of excluding employees with certain disorders from promotions.[27] The moral for employers in light of this discussion is that "personality tests" should be checked thoroughly to see if some mental impairment may not be revealed through the use of those tests. Such a check may call into question whether the test should be used at all, as taking out certain questions may compromise the validity of the entire test. Nevertheless, keeping in those questions may ensure the validity of the test but result in liability for the employer per *Karraker.*

The ADA allows medical exams of applicants *after* a conditional job offer by the employer. A medical exam or medical inquiry that tests for anything can be done after an offer of employment has been made and the offer is conditioned upon the results of the medical exam.[28] However, if employment is denied to an individual based upon the medical exam, the basis of the denial must be job-related and consistent with business necessity, and the performance of the job cannot be accomplished with reasonable accommodations.[29] What is "job-related" must be determined by further litigation. However, considering the ADA's focus on the individual and on particular jobs, it could well be that "job-related" will refer to the specific job at issue and not to any broad definitions of jobs. Clearly, preventive lawyering demands that the specific job at issue be looked to rather than the broad class of jobs in assessing job-relatedness.

While preemployment medical exams have broad latitude, the results can only be used against an individual where it is determined that the test is job-related, shows that the person cannot perform the essential job functions with reasonable accommodations, and is consistent with business necessity.[30] As mentioned earlier, a current employee can be requested to undergo a medical exam providing it is job-related and consistent with business necessity.[31]

Finally, the ADA requires that medical information obtained on an employee or prospective employee be kept confidential.[32] To that end, medical information cannot be kept in regular personnel files,[33] and the confidentiality obligation of the employer extends even after employment has terminated.[34] An individual can voluntarily disclose his or her own medical information as long as the disclosure is truly voluntary—that is, the employee has not been requested, persuaded, coerced or otherwise pressured to disclose the information.[35] It should be noted that just because the individual self-discloses does not mean the employer is then free to disclose medical information at its whim.

There are also exceptions to the confidentiality provisions. They are as follows:

- Supervisors and managers may be told about necessary restrictions on the work or duties of the employee and about necessary accommodations.
- First aid and safety personnel may be told if the disability might require emergency treatment.
- Government officials investigating compliance with the ADA must be given relevant information on request.
- Employers may give information to state worker's compensation offices, state second-injury funds, or worker's compensation insurance carriers in accordance with state worker's compensation laws.
- Employers may use the information for insurance purposes.[36]

NOTES

1. EEOC Guidance on Pre-Employment Disability-Related Inquiries and Medical Examinations Under the ADA.
2. *Id.*
3. *Id.*
4. *Id.*
5. *Id.*
6. Karraker v. Rent-A-Center, Inc., 411 F.3d 831 (7th Cir. 2005).
7. *Id.* at 833.
8. *Id.*
9. *Id.*
10. *Id.*
11. *Id.*
12. *Id.* at 834.
13. *Id.*
14. *Id.*
15. *Id.*
16. *Id.*
17. *Id.* at 835.
18. The EEOC's Enforcement Guidance on Disability-Related Inquiries and Medical Examinations Under the ADA is *available at* http://www.eeoc.gov/policy/docs/guidance-inquiries.html.

19. *Karraker,* 411 F.3d at 835, citing to the EEOC's 1995 enforcement guidance on preemployment disability-related questions and medical examinations.
20. *Id.* at 835.
21. *Id.* at 835-36.
22. *Id.* at 836.
23. *Id.*
24. *Id.*
25. *Id.* at 836-37.
26. *Id.* at 837.
27. *Id.*
28. 29 C.F.R. § 1630.14(b).
29. 29 C.F.R. § 1630.14(b)(3).
30. *Id.*
31. 42 U.S.C. § 12112(d)(4)(A).
32. 42 U.S.C. § 12112(d)(2)(B).
33. EEOC Guidance on Pre-Employment Disability-Related Inquiries and Medical Examinations Under the ADA.
34. *Id.*
35. *Id.*
36. *Id.*

The ADA and Health Insurance

6

THE ADA APPLIES TO ALL BENEFITS, conditions, and privileges of employment as well as employment decisions.[1] Therefore, how might the ADA apply to insurance benefits offered under a health insurance plan? Back in 1993, the EEOC issued Guidelines on the ADA and Health Insurance,[2] and considerable time was spent discussing these guidelines in the first edition of this book. However, as of this writing, Spring 2006, the guidelines have not been received well by the courts. There is one case that explicitly mentions these guidelines,[3] but it does not fare well when Sheppardized. In fact, when the case is Sheppardized, you find the court explicitly says the EEOC guidelines on disability distinctions in health insurance are entitled to no deference, and that is the nicest thing the court has to say about them.[4] What has happened over the years is that the courts are more likely to give the insurance company wide latitude in determining how its policy is to be configured.[5] Thus, while the first edition of this book spent considerable time on the ADA and the particulars of health insurance, one wonders about the utility of doing so now in light of how the law has evolved in this area.

NOTES

1. 42 U.S.C. § 12,112(a).
2. EEOC Interim Policy Guidance on ADA and Health Insurance.
3. *See* Anderson v. Gus Mayer Boston Store, 924 F. Supp. 763 (E.D. Tex. 1996).
4. Weyer v. Twentieth Century Fox Film Corp., 198 F.3d 1104, 1117 (9th Cir. 1999).
5. *See* Doe v. Mutual of Omaha Ins. Co., 179 F.3d 557 (7th Cir. 1999).

ADA and the Public Sector (Title II)

7

EMPLOYMENT CONCERNS

TITLE II OF THE ADA applies to governmental entities, including employment, programs, activities, and benefits.[1] Title II is enforced not by the EEOC, but by the Department of Justice (DOJ).[2] If a governmental entity has more than fifteen employees and a discrimination suit is filed against it, is the governmental entity subject to Title I or II or both? For example, if an agency has more than fifteen employees, the EEOC regulations apply, although the DOJ has enforcement authority.[3] One lower court did hold that Title II does not apply to employment; however, that decision was reversed by the Eleventh Circuit on appeal.[4]

Title II of the ADA also imposes some additional requirements on the governmental employer. For example, if the public entity has over fifty employees, it must have an internal grievance procedure for handling complaints of disability-based discrimination and a designated person to be the ADA coordinator.[5] Since many public entities already have a 504 coordinator because they receive federal funds, it is only natural to make that person the ADA coordinator as well.

While a grievance procedure is mandated for governmental entities of over fifty employees, an entity with under fifty employees may elect to have such a procedure in order to prevent problems. Having the procedure in place gives the entity a chance to resolve a dispute before it escalates into protracted litigation. It also gives the entity the chance to discover the concerns of the aggrieved employee and allows the plaintiff to vent his or her feelings. Finally, it may represent the only chance for the entity to head off a courtroom battle, because a person does have a private cause of action under Title II of the ADA,[6] and a plaintiff need not exhaust administrative remedies before filing suit.[7]

PROGRAM ACCESSIBILITY

A reading of the Title II regulations reveals that there is virtually nothing about employment contained in them; instead, the focus of the regulations is on accessing governmental programs and activities. Thus, when dealing with a person with a disability's right to access a governmental entity, three other questions must be answered: 1) Does the person have a disability as defined by the ADA? 2) Is the person otherwise qualified? and 3) If the answer to both is yes, one must determine whether the governmental program or activity is readily accessible to the individual with the particular disability.

Since the definition of a disability is the same under all titles of the ADA, the second question can be considered first. Under Title II of the ADA, "otherwise qualified" has a different meaning than it does under Title I. In the context of Title II, a person with a disabling condition or disability is deemed to be otherwise qualified if he or she can, with or without reasonable modifications to rules, policies, or practices; the removal of architectural, communication, or transportation barriers; or the provision of auxiliary aids and services, meet the essential eligibility requirements for the receipt of services or the participation in programs or activities provided by a public entity.[8] This definition raises two more very significant questions: What is a reasonable modification, and what constitutes a program?

A reasonable modification to a program, benefit, or activity is whatever does not constitute an undue burden or a fundamental alteration in the program.[9] Proving an undue burden is very difficult,[10] and thus the governmental entity might be more successful arguing that the program would be fundamentally altered by the needed accommodation. The governmental entity is under a powerful disincentive to take the position that a modification would be an undue burden because where one exists, the CEO of the public entity must certify as such, and then all changes up until the point of undue burden must be paid for by the public entity.[11]

Program accessibility is a critical concept to Title II of the ADA. Title II analysis frequently depends on the definition of a *program* for two reasons. First, a Title II entity does not have to make an accommodation if it will fundamentally alter the program.[12] Second, under Title II of the ADA, existing facilities built before January 26, 1992, do not have to be accessible; only the program does.[13] For example, an English class is offered on the second floor of a building with no elevator. A mobility-impaired person wants to take that class. There is no reason that class or an identical one taught by a different instructor could not be offered at an accessible location. That said, it does pay to remember that facilities built after the effective date of the ADA must be readily accessible to persons with disabilities.[14] Thus, the question becomes what constitutes a program. As a preventive law measure, consider the following when trying to determine this issue:

1. Review the self-evaluation plan (a document that assesses all of a Title II entity's programs and reviews their accessibility) to see the governmental entity's view of what a program is.
2. Consider the commonalities in the delivery of the program's service, as programs are often built around a common set of services to a defined set of clientele.
3. Consider the common usage of the term *program* to the people in the governmental entity; what their particular program is may be fairly obvious to them. For example, in the mental health and mental retardation field, it is common to have such programs as case management, cooperative living, client-support services, mental retardation residential care, etc., and everyone in the profession understands precisely what is being referred to.
4. Consult competent legal counsel to help determine what constitutes a program.

THE CRITICAL NATURE OF ASSESSING THE PROGRAM AND ITS ESSENTIAL REQUIREMENTS

How a program is defined and its essential eligibility requirements can be critical to the outcome of a case. That was certainly true in *Concerned Parents to Save Dreher Park Center v. City of W. Palm Beach*[15] and in *Easley v. Snider*.[16]

(Sheppardize)

In *Concerned Parents*, the city of West Palm Beach had established state-of-the-art recreational facilities, the Dreher Park Center, for persons with disabilities living in West Palm Beach and in the surrounding area.[17] Due to poor fiscal management, budget cuts became necessary, and the city elected to eliminate the recreational facilities.[18] A group of concerned parents banded together and sought a preliminary injunction under Title II of the ADA and under the Florida Constitution to prohibit the city from terminating the recreation programs.[19] Two issues were before the court: What was the program at issue, and what were the essential eligibility requirements of that program? The court found that the program was the entire network of activities and services, and declined to adopt a more specific definition of programs that involved physical abilities.[20] The court also said the essential eligibility requirement for the program as defined above was simply the request for the benefits of the program.[21] With the program and the essential eligibility requirements thus determined, the court quite logically held that the city's action denied persons with disabilities access to the city's program and violated the ADA.[22]

Finally, the court in *Dreher* did not accept two defenses made by the city. First, the city claimed that it was important that the discrimination was not intentional.[23] The court dismissed that argument by saying intent was not the issue; the issue was whether the decision to terminate the programs for persons with disabilities had the effect of discriminating against persons with disabilities.[24] Second, the city said its decision was in keeping with the spirit of the ADA, as it would enable everyone to participate in an integrated setting.[25] The court dismissed that argument as well by noting that the ADA requires that the setting be the most appropriate for persons with disabilities and that the "ADA contemplates separate programming where necessary to provide qualified individuals with disabilities the aids and benefits of services that are as effective as those provided to others."[26]

The lesson from *Dreher* is that plaintiff lawyers need to define the program as broadly as possible, while defense lawyers need to define it as narrowly as possible.

Easley v. Snider is a bit different from *Dreher*. In *Easley*, the program was very clear, but the issues were the program's essential eligibility requirements and whether those requirements were a subterfuge for discrimination. In *Easley*, two persons with disabilities sought an injunction against the state of Pennsylvania for denying their inclusion in an attendant care program.[27] The rules of that program required that the participants be mentally alert.[28] Neither plaintiff met this requirement, and they brought suit challenging the requirement as being discriminatory in violation of the ADA.[29] The plaintiffs won at the district court level and the state of Pennsylvania appealed. The Third Circuit reversed.[30] In its ruling, the court noted that the rules for the program demanded that the person who participates in the program be able to do four things, two of which were critical: be capable of selecting, supervising and, if needed, firing an attendant, and be capable of managing their own financial and legal affairs.[31]

The court then turned to the policies of the program stated by the Pennsylvania General Assembly. Again, two of those findings are relevant in this discussion:

1. Priority recipients of attendant care services under this Act shall be those mentally alert but severely physically disabled who are at the greatest risk of being in an institutional setting; and
2. Recipients of attendant care have the right to make decisions about, direct the provision of, and control their attendant care services. This includes but is not limited to hiring, training, managing, paying, and firing of an attendant.[32]

Given the parameters of the program, the court went on to note that eliminating a mental alertness requirement would fundamentally alter the very nature of the program, which the ADA does not require.[33] Finally, the court stated that it would consider, in determining if a program of a governmental entity discriminates, whether the plaintiff meets the program's requirements in spite of the disability and whether a reasonable accommodation could allow that person to receive the program's essential benefits.[34] Further, when determining whether an accommodation would allow the applicant to receive the benefit, the court is not to rely solely on the stated benefits, because programs may attempt to define the benefit in a way that effectively denies otherwise qualified disabled individuals the access to which they are entitled.[35] The language revealing skepticism about relying on stated benefits is very significant, because in cases arising under the Rehabilitation Act of 1973, it was not unusual for courts to give deference to governmental entities in determining what the program was.[36]

ACTIVITY ACCESSIBILITY

Not all cases involving Title II concern access to a program. They may deal with access to an activity. Consider this scenario.

> A public high school student has cerebral palsy. Her older sister is a cheerleader. Her sister is able to convince the school to allow the student with cerebral palsy to join the cheerleading squad as an honorary cheerleader. The student is made a part of the team and completes her duties. Fast-forward to the next year: The older sister has graduated and the younger girl wants to be a cheerleader again. The school says no, since she can't do the things that cheerleaders do—gymnastics, tumbling, etc. She brings suit under the ADA.[37]

As this is a public high school, the applicable section of the ADA is Title II, which applies to governmental entities, including employment, its programs, *activities,* and benefits.[38] In analyzing this situation, several questions have to be asked. Does the cheerleader have a disability? Cerebral palsy is certainly a disability, because it is a physical impairment that substantially limits, even under *Toyota Motor,* various major life activities, including speech and walking. Also, due to the nature of the disability, mitigating measures are not an issue. Is cheerleading an activity? Certainly, it is common to think of cheerleading as one of the activities offered by the school. Is the cheerleader otherwise qualified? In light of the definition of *otherwise qualified,*[39] one must determine the essential eligibility requirements of the activity. Is it tumbling? Cheering? Dancing?

The essential eligibility requirements of cheerleading at this school could only be determined through discovery. Not all cheerleading units have the same requirements. Some units focus on gymnastics, while others focus predominantly on cheering. A videotape of the cheerleading unit in action over the course of the prior season would be very helpful. Such a videotape probably exists, because most football teams tape their games. In assessing the essential eligibility requirements, it is instructive to first assess what is fundamental to carrying out that activity. In that way, determining essential eligibility requirements of an activity is analogous to determining the essential functions of a job.

Once the "essential functions"—essential eligibility requirements—of cheerleading have been determined, the next question is whether the cheerleader is able to meet those requirements with or without reasonable modification in the activity. If tumbling is essential to the cheering activity, there is probably no reasonable modification that can be put into place. But if cheering is essential to the cheering activity, there are probably any number of reasonable modifications that can be made.

Even if gymnastics is an essential eligibility requirement of cheering at this school, the matter is not necessarily resolved. It is entirely possible that the plaintiff might be able to do the essential activities with or without reasonable modifications if she were in a different section of the cheerleading unit—perhaps the pom pon squad.

This case has an interesting postscript. The case settled, and the cheerleader was allowed to try out without performing the tumbling and gymnastics part. The settlement raises the issue of why the school district allowed the cheerleader to try out without completing the tumbling and gymnastic requirements, because if tumbling and gymnastics were an essential eligibility requirement of cheering at the school, the school district was under no obligation to modify the tryouts.[40] A different conclusion would be in order if tumbling were a marginal function of cheering at this school.[41] In the latter case, a waiver of these tryout requirements would have certainly been appropriate. Of course, it is entirely possible that other factors entered into the settlement, such as fear of losing at trial, the cost of litigation, and the like.

ZONING

Consider the following:

> An entity runs a substance abuse program. It wants to move to a downtown location, which causes an uproar in the surrounding community. At the preliminary hearing, the application for

the zoning variance is approved, but it is later appealed. The appellate level that hears the zoning request succumbs to political pressure and denies the zoning variance. The entity sues, alleging that the action of denying the zoning variance violates Title II of the ADA.

This hypothetical scenario was the fact pattern in *Innovative Health System v. City of White Plains*, a case that came before the Second Circuit Court of Appeals.[42] The issues before the court were twofold: First, were decisions made pursuant to zoning regulations subject to suit under the ADA? Second, could an entity serving persons with disabilities, rather than just the persons with disabilities being served, bring suit for violations of Title II of the ADA?

Turning to the first issue, the Second Circuit noted, as discussed earlier, that the ADA does not define "services, programs, or activities."[43] However, the court looked for guidance to Section 508 of the Rehabilitation Act, which defined a program or activity of a governmental entity as all of the operations of the specific entities.[44] The court also looked to the dictionary definition of the term *activity*, which described it as a natural or normal function of operation.[45] Finally, the court looked to the *Department of Justice Technical Assistance Manual* and to the Preamble to the Department of Justice regulations on Title II of the ADA, which specifically mentioned zoning as one of the activities covered under Title II.[46]

With regard to the second issue, the Second Circuit held that Title II of the ADA specifically allows any person alleging discrimination on the basis of disability to bring suit, and that such language was consistent with congressional intent to allow private actions as broadly as possible under the U.S. Constitution.[47]

Having found that the service provider could bring the suit and that zoning is subject to Title II of the ADA, the court held that, based on the evidence of the public hearings, the denial of the zoning variance was nothing more than discrimination based on disability due to stereotypical attitudes.[48]

SOVEREIGN IMMUNITY

In the first edition of this book, I talked about sovereign immunity and what might or might not happen vis-á-vis the ADA. In the first edition,

I set forth several reasons why I thought the Supreme Court would hold that Congress properly waived sovereign immunity of the states under the ADA. Among the reasons I gave were: 1) The ADA waives sovereign immunity;[49] 2) The Supreme Court at the time the first edition went to press had considered several ADA cases. While none dealt with sovereign immunity, the cases were written as if waiving sovereign immunity were a possibility; and 3) The Preamble to the ADA, which is quite sweeping.[50] One possible effect of that Preamble would be to put persons with disabilities in a higher equal protection class, thereby justifying Congress to enact a comprehensive law from which the states could be sued for private damages. Was I right? The answer is that with respect to employment matters, it did not work out that way—that is, Congress did not properly waive sovereign immunity.[51] With respect to non-employment matters, whether sovereign immunity was effectively waived is subject to a case-by-case analysis.[52]

Before proceeding further, it is necessary to briefly cover the standards of review in equal protection jurisprudence. Equal protection jurisprudence has three different levels of review: strict scrutiny, intermediate scrutiny, and rational basis.[53] The highest level of review is race-based classifications, "suspect class."[54] The second level of review is gender-based classifications, an "intermediate level" of review.[55] The last level of review is "rational basis"—that is, for everyone else.[56] The way the system works is that classification is everything. If a group of people fall into a "suspect class," it is virtually impossible for the government's discrimination against that class to stand (the only exception I am aware of being the case that set forth the "suspect class" classification).[57] If a group of people fall into the intermediate review classification, gender, then it is possible for the government discrimination to stand, but there would have to be very good reasons to allow it to proceed.[58] The final level of review is "rational basis." If a group of people fall into this level of review, then the government discrimination will in all probability stand because the law just has to be one that a rational legislator would make.[59] Hence, the more discrimination a group of people has suffered (the higher class of review they fall in), the more comprehensive Congress can get in redressing the discrimination faced by that group.

With respect to sovereign immunity in employment, the controlling case is *Board of Trustees of University of Alabama v. Garrett,* hereafter *Garrett.*[60] In *Garrett,* two separate plaintiffs who worked

for the state of Alabama, one as a nurse at the University of Alabama
Birmingham Hospital and the other as a security officer at the department of youth services, sought money damages under the Americans
with Disabilities Act as a result of alleged discrimination based on their
disabilities.[61] The issue before the court was whether these plaintiffs had
the right to sue the state via a private cause of action for money damages.[62] The Court, in an opinion written by Chief Justice Rehnquist,
reasoned as follows. First, the Court noted that the Eleventh Amendment
applied to the situation where citizens of one state sue that state for money
damages.[63] The Court also noted that to hold a waiver of sovereign immunity valid, they had to find that Congress was carrying out the enforcement provisions of section 5 of the Fourteenth Amendment to the
U.S. Constitution.[64] Whether those enforcement provisions are satisfied
vis-à-vis a statutory scheme depends entirely on what equal protection
class the plaintiff(s) at issue fall in.[65]

Second, the Court cited two cases, *Cleburne v. Cleburne Living
Center, Inc.*[66] and *Heller v. Doe,*[67] for the proposition that persons with
disabilities were in the "rational basis class."[68] At this point, the plaintiffs effectively lost their case, because being in the rational basis class
meant that the ADA statutory scheme was an overly comprehensive
way to redress the wrongs faced by persons who fell within that class.[69]
It is unfortunate that the Court relied on these two cases for the proposition just stated, because neither case actually held as such. In *Cleburne,*
it is true that the Court said there was no rational basis for the government to discriminate against an independent living center that wanted
to locate in a particular area of town.[70] However, *Cleburne* can hardly
be said to be a typical "rational basis" review case. In *Cleburne* the
Court only concluded that there was no rational basis for the governmental action after a searching discussion of how government had
been quite aggressive in trying to serve the needs of persons with mental retardation.[71] In fact, Justice Marshall, in an opinion joined by Justices Brennan and Blackmun, where he concurred and dissented, makes
the point that the Court's reasoning does not resemble rational basis
review at all because far too much attention is paid in the opinion to
the rights of persons with mental retardation and to mental retardation
in general.[72] Justice Marshall thought it would be more accurate to call
the level of review of the majority in Cleburne "second order rational
basis."[73] Turning to *Heller,* the Court specifically noted that it was not
asked to decide what equal protection class persons with disabilities

fell in; rather, the parties had already stipulated that persons with disabilities were in the rational basis class.[74]

Third, the court found that the legislative record of the ADA failed to show that the states had discriminated against persons with disabilities in employment in an irrational manner over time.[75]

Finally, two other points are worth noting. First, the Court said municipalities were not immune from liability for a private cause of action seeking money damages, as they were not a sovereign.[76] Second, the Court noted its decision applied only to money damages and not to a plaintiff seeking equitable relief against the state.[77]

The other case dealing with sovereign immunity is *Tennessee v. Lane.*[78] *Lane* is in some ways is hard to reconcile with *Garrett.* That the outcome was different is entirely due to Justice O'Connor, as she was the only Justice in the majority in both cases. In *Lane,* two paraplegics sued the state of Tennessee for their inability to access courthouses.[79] One of the plaintiffs could not access the courthouse where he had to make an appearance for a criminal case he was involved in.[80] The other plaintiff was a stenographer and simply could not go to certain job assignments because the job assignments were not accessible to mobility-impaired individuals.[81] They brought suit against the state of Tennessee for money damages and equitable relief alleging violations of the Americans with Disabilities Act.[82] The issue before the Court was the same as the issue in *Garrett,* except the question of whether Congress properly waived sovereign immunity involved Title II of the ADA rather than Title I.[83] In an opinion by Justice Stevens, the Supreme Court held that Congress did properly waive sovereign immunity of the states with respect to Title II of the ADA, but such a waiver depended upon the facts of each individual case.[84]

The Court took great pains to distinguish *Garrett* from the case at bar. First, they noted that Title II of the ADA seeks to enforce a variety of basic constitutional guarantees, which are subject to a more searching level of judicial review.[85] They then proceeded to note some of those rights, including access to the courts, the right to be present at all stages of the trial where the defendants' absence might frustrate the fairness of the proceeding, the right to afford civil litigants a meaningful opportunity to be heard by removing barriers to their full participation in judicial proceedings, the right of a criminal defendant to a jury composed of a fair cross-section of the community, and the right of the public to access criminal proceedings.[86]

Second, the Court said that Title II of the ADA was enacted against a backdrop of pervasive discrimination against people with disabilities in the administration of state services and programs, which included the systematic deprivation of fundamental rights.[87] Some of the fundamental rights that states have limited for people with disabilities included the right to vote, the right to marry, and the right to serve as jurors. [88] The Court also noted the unconstitutional treatment of persons with disabilities by state agencies in many different settings, including unjustified commitment, abuse and neglect of persons with disabilities committed to state mental health hospitals, and irrational discrimination in zoning decisions.[89] Finally, the Court noted that the decisions of other courts document a pattern of unequal treatment in the administration of many kinds of public services, programs, and activities, such as the penal system, public education, and voting.[90]

Third, the Court mentioned it recently had decided *Nevada Department of Human Resources v. Hibbs*, 538 U.S. 721 (2003), where it held that the Family and Medical Leave Act waived sovereign immunity of the states, and that the record of constitutional violations in *Lane* far exceeded the record in *Hibbs*.[91] This led the Court to conclude that where basic rights are involved, the standard of review should be at least as searching if not more searching than the review for sex-based classifications.[92] In short, the Court concluded that Title II of the ADA was not out of proportion to the harm meant to be redressed, and therefore sovereign immunity was properly waived.[93]

The next portion of *Lane* is unprecedented. The Court said there was nothing in the case law that required the Court to consider Title II of the ADA as a whole with respect to what equal protection class persons with disabilities fall in.[94] After making this statement, the Court held that the ADA is proper legislation vis-à-vis the enforcement clause of the Fourteenth Amendment to the U.S. Constitution with respect to judicial services, noting a long history of unequal treatment for persons with disabilities in the administration of judicial services despite legislative efforts to remedy the problem.[95]

Finally, the very last paragraph of the majority opinion concludes that Title II of the ADA as it applies to the class of cases pertaining to the *fundamental right* (emphasis added) of access to the court is a valid exercise of the enforcement clause of the Fourteenth Amendment, and therefore sovereign immunity was properly waived.[96]

So where does this leave us? The Supreme Court in *Lane* at various points in the majority opinion uses the terms "basic constitutional guarantees,"[97] "basic rights,"[98] "class of cases implicating judicial services,"[99] and "fundamental rights."[100] Clearly, the most narrow way to read *Lane* is to say that *Lane* applies only where a case involves judicial services. Yet a close reading of the decision suggests that *Lane* must expand to other rights as well because of its reasoning, discussed above, and the broad rights terminology used in the case. In short, it would seem disability rights advocates have an opening under *Lane* to argue that sovereign immunity is waived regardless of whether a state consents whenever you have rights involving "basic constitutional guarantees," "basic rights," or "fundamental rights." In any event, to this author's knowledge, it is unprecedented for a class of people in equal protection jurisprudence to have their classification vary depending on the facts.

It appeared that the U.S. Supreme Court would address the question of how far the waiver of sovereign immunity vis-á-vis Title II extended when it took the case of *Goodman v. Georgia*. While it is true that the Supreme Court has already decided that states can be sued for violating Title II of the ADA with respect to prisons, they had not decided whether such suits could seek money damages.[101] The *Goodman* decision could have well turned on just how far the Court wanted to go in interpreting *Lane*. Would it stick to judicial services, or would it explore the case law pertaining to "basic constitutional guarantees," "basic rights," or "fundamental rights"? It turns out there were two surprises in the decision handed down by the Supreme Court in this case. First, it was unanimous.[102] Second, it sidestepped these issues entirely by holding that sovereign immunity was waived under Title II of the ADA where the violation of the ADA alleged also rose to the level of a constitutional violation.[103] It reserved for a further time how the case-by-case analysis of Title II set forth in *Lane* might play itself out.[104]

REMEDIES

While a full range of remedies are available to the person aggrieved by a violation of Title II of the ADA,[105] the question arose as to whether punitive damages were available to a person aggrieved by Title II itself. The Supreme Court was presented with that very question in

Barnes v. Gorman.[106] In *Barnes*, a paraplegic confined to a wheelchair and lacking voluntary control over his lower torso, including the bladder, was arrested for fighting with a bouncer at a Kansas City, Missouri, nightclub.[107] While waiting for the police van to pick him up, he was denied permission to use the restroom to empty his urine bag.[108] The van that arrived was not equipped to take his wheelchair.[109] The officers removed him from his wheelchair and used a seat belt and his own belt to fasten him to a narrow bench in the rear of the van.[110] During the ride to the police station, he released his seat belt, fearing excessive pressure on his urine bag.[111] Consequently, the other belt came loose and he fell to the floor of the van, rupturing his urine bag and injuring his shoulder and back.[112] Since he could not be lifted, the driver, the only officer in the van, fastened him to a support in the van for the remainder of the trip.[113] As a result of all this, he suffered serious medical problems, including a bladder infection, serious lower back pain, and uncontrollable spasms in his paralyzed areas, leaving him unable to work full-time.[114] He then brought suit against the Kansas City Board of Police Commissioners, the chief of police, and the officer who drove the van, claiming that he had been discriminated against in violation of Title II of the ADA because he was not reasonably accommodated in his transport.[115] At trial, he won over $1 million in compensatory damages and $1.2 million in punitive damages.[116] However, the district court threw out the punitive damages award, holding punitive damages were neither available under Title II of the ADA nor, for that matter, under section 504 of the Rehabilitation Act of 1973 (a law prohibiting discrimination against persons with disabilities by an entity receiving federal funds), which he also sued under.[117] The district court decision throwing out the punitive damages award was reversed by the Eighth Circuit and an appeal was taken to the U.S. Supreme Court.[118]

In holding that punitive damages were not allowed in a private cause of action brought under Title II of the ADA and section 504 of the Rehabilitation Act of 1973, the Court reasoned as follows. First, the Court noted that private causes of action were available under Title II of the ADA and under the Rehabilitation Act of 1973 and that the remedies for both were the same based upon how the statutes were set up.[119] Second, because the ADA and Rehabilitation Acts were tied to the spending power of Congress, the legitimacy of Congress's power to legislate rested on whether the recipient voluntarily and knowingly accepted the terms of the contract.[120] Third, since the acts did not mention punitive damages, the Court asked itself what would be the normal expectation for the recipient of a contract.[121] Because causes of action for breach of contract do not allow for punitive damages, the Court found that it was not reasonable to expect the contracting party to believe punitive damages could be imposed upon it for violating Title II of the ADA or section 504 of the Rehabilitation Act of 1973.[122] As punitive damages could be a disaster for a public entity, the Court believed that the public entity would never have accepted federal funding if punitive damage liability were a possibility to that entity.[123]

NOTES

1. 42 U.S.C. § 12132.
2. 42 U.S.C. § 12134(a).
3. 28 C.F.R. § 35.140(b)(1).
4. Bledsoe v. Palm Beach Soil and Water Conservation District, 942 F. Supp. 1439 (S.D. Fla. 1996), *reversed on appeal,* 133 F.3d 816 (11th Cir. 1998).
5. 28 C.F.R. § 35.107.
6. *See* 42 U.S.C. § 12133.
7. Peterson v. Univ. of Wis., 818 F. Supp. 1276, 1277 (W.D. Wis. 1993).
8. 28 C.F.R. § 35.104.
9. 28 C.F.R. § 35.130(b)(7).
10. *See* Penn. Prot. and Advocacy Inc. v. Penn. Dep't of Public Welfare, 402 F.3d 374 (3d Cir. 2005).
11. 28 C.F.R. § 35.150(3).
12. 28 C.F.R. § 35.130(b)(7).
13. 28 C.F.R. § 35.130(a)(1).
14. 28 C.F.R. § 35.151(a).
15. Concerned Parents to Save Dreher Park Center v. City of West Palm Beach, 846 F. Supp. 986 (S.D. Fla. 1994), *consent decree entered* at 853 F. Supp. 424 (S.D. Fla. 1994), *final judgment entered* at 884 F. Supp. 487 (S.D. Fla. 1994).
16. Easley v. Snider, 36 F.3d 297 (3d Cir. 1994).
17. *Concerned Parents,* 846 F. Supp. at 988.
18. *Id.* at 989.
19. *Id.*
20. *Id.* at 990.
21. *Id.*
22. *Id.* at 989 n.8
23. *Id.* at 991.
24. *Id.*
25. *Id.*
26. *Id.*

27. *Easley*, 36 F.3d at 299.
28. *Id.*
29. *Id.*
30. *Id.*
31. *Id.*
32. *Id.* at 300.
33. *Id.* at 302-04.
34. *Id.* at 302.
35. *Id.*
36. *E.g.,* Southeastern Community College v. Davis, 442 U.S. 397 (1979).
37. *See* Goren, William D., *On Gymnastics and Cheerleading: An Instructive ADA Case*, XV The Sports Lawyer 3-4 (Spring 1997).
38. 42 U.S.C. § 12132.
39. 28 C.F.R. § 35.104.
40. *Easley*, 36 F.3d at 302-04.
41. *Id.*
42. Innovative Health System v. City of White Plains, 117 F.3d 37 (2d Cir. 1997).
43. *Id.* at 44.
44. *Id.*
45. *Id.*
46. *Id.* at 45.
47. *Id.* at 47.
48. *Id.* at 48-49.
49. 42 U.S.C. § 2000d-7.
50. *See* 42 U.S.C. § 12101.
51. *See generally* Bd. of Trustees of Univ. of Ala. v. Garrett, 531 U.S. 356 (2001).
52. *See generally* Tenn. v. Lane, 541 U.S. 509 (2004).
53. *E.g.,* City of Cleburne v. Cleburne Living Center, 473 U.S. 432, 439-41 (1985).
54. *Id.* at 440.
55. *Id.*
56. *Id.* at 440-41.
57. *Id.* at 440.
58. *Id.* at 440-41.
59. *See id.* at 440-41.
60. Bd. of Trustees of Univ. of Ala. v. Garrett, 531 U.S. 356 (2001).
61. *Id.* at 362.
62. *Id.* at 360.
63. *Id.* at 364.
64. *Id.*
65. *See id.* at 364, 374.
66. Cleburne v. Cleburne Living Center, Inc., 473 U.S. 432 (1985).
67. Heller v. Doe, 509 U.S. 312 (1993).

68. *Garrett,* at 366.
69. *Id.* at 372.
70. *Cleburne,* 473 U.S. at 446-50.
71. *Id.* at 443-47.
72. *Id.* at 456, 458 (Marshall, J., concurring and dissenting in part).
73. *Id.*
74. Heller v. Doe, 509 U.S. 312, 319 (1993). *See also* William D. Goren, *Counterpoint: Congress Did Properly Waive the States' Sovereign Immunity in Enacting the ADA,* DCBA Brief (Jan. 2001), http://www.dcba.org/brief/janissue/2001/art10101.htm.
75. *Garrett,* 531 U.S. at 368.
76. *Id.* at 369.
77. *Id.* at 374 n.9.
78. Tenn. v. Lane, 541 U.S. 509 (2004).
79. *Id.* at 513.
80. *Id.* at 513-14.
81. *Id.* at 514.
82. *Id.*
83. *Id.* at 515.
84. *Id.* at 529-30.
85. *Id.* at 522-23.
86. *Id.*
87. *Id.* at 524.
88. *Id.*
89. *Id.* at 524-25.
90. *Id.* at 525.
91. *Id.* at 527-28.
92. *Id.* at 529.
93. *Id.* at 533.
94. *Id.* at 530.
95. *Id.* at 531.
96. *Id.* at 534.
97. *Id.* at 522.
98. *Id.* at 529.
99. *Id.* at 531.
100. *Id.* at 524, 534.
101. Penn. Dep't of Corr. v. Yeskey, 524 U.S. 206, 212-13 (1998).
102. United States v. Georgia, 126 S. Ct. 877 (2006).
103. *Id.* at 882.
104. *Id.*
105. Barnes v. Gorman, 536 U.S. 181, 184-85 (2002).
106. *See generally id.*
107. *Id.* at 183.
108. *Id.*
109. *Id.*

110. *Id.*
111. *Id.*
112. *Id.*
113. *Id.*
114. *Id.* at 184.
115. *Id.*
116. *Id.*
117. *Id.*
118. *Id.*
119. *Id.* at 185.
120. *Id.* at 186.
121. *Id.* at 187.
122. *Id.* at 187-88.
123. *Id.* at 188.

Places of Public Accommodations and Commercial Facilities

8

UNLIKE TITLE II OF THE ADA, an entity covered by Title III of the ADA must have each of its facilities readily accessible to persons with disabilities. Program accessibility is not a concept found in Title III of the ADA. If a building built before the advent of the ADA is involved, then the business has to make only structural changes that are readily achievable.[1] Where auxiliary aids and services are involved, changes must be made unless to do so would constitute an undue burden or a fundamental alteration in the nature of the goods, services, facilities, privileges, advantages, or accommodations being offered.[2] Finally, if there is an alteration in the facility or a new building is built, very specific architectural accessibility guidelines must be satisfied.[3] These general principles give rise to several questions:

- What businesses are subject to Title III of the ADA, and are there any exemptions?
- What is meant by "readily achievable"?
- What is an auxiliary aid and service?
- What is meant by "undue burden"?
- What constitutes an alteration in a facility?

71

- Does Title III apply when a person with a disability wants to use a business that does not rely on a physical location (for example, terms of an insurance policy, direct mail business, doctor's office for consultation, buying a product on the Internet, etc.)?

Title III of the ADA applies to all places of "public accommodations."[4] A place of public accommodation is a facility operated by a *private* entity that affects interstate commerce and falls into any of the following categories:

1. Places of lodging
2. Establishments serving food and drink
3. Places of exhibition and entertainment
4. Places of public gathering, such as a museum or library
5. Sales or rental establishments
6. Service establishments
7. Specified public transportation
   a. Terminals
   b. Depots
8. Public display or collection
9. Places of recreation (parks, etc.)
10. Places of education
11. Social service center
12. Place of exercise or recreation (athletic in nature)[5]

Two other significant points regarding Title III bear mentioning. First, religious entities are exempt from Title III coverage.[6] For example, many private schools are religious in nature or run by religious organizations and therefore are exempt from Title III of the ADA, even though places of education are generally covered.[7] Second, it is entirely conceivable that a business not otherwise subject to the ADA could have a portion of its premises covered by the ADA. Apartment complexes are an example. Apartment complexes are not subject to Title III of the ADA as a place of public accommodation, but they are subject to the federal and state fair housing acts. Nevertheless, the area or office where the public goes to lease an apartment would be subject to Title III of the ADA on the grounds that it is a service establishment or a sales and rental establishment.[8] Consider the following scenario.

A business is in an existing facility built before the ADA went into effect and is considered a place of public accommodation under Title III of the ADA. An architect reviews the facility and determines that there are numerous ADA compliance issues. What are the obligations of the business to make changes to comply with the ADA regulations on architectural barriers? What if the business leases the facility? Does the landlord have ADA obligations?

With respect to the existing facility question, the obligation exists to make whatever changes are readily achievable. The Department of Justice defines "readily achievable" as meaning without much difficulty or expense[9] and lists several factors to consider in making the determination. They are:

1. The nature and cost of the action needed.
2. The overall financial resources of the site or sites involved in the action.
3. The number of persons employed at the site.
4. The effect on expenses and resources.
5. Legitimate safety requirements that are necessary for safe operation, including crime prevention measures.
6. If applicable:
   a. The geographic separateness and the administrative or fiscal relationship of the site or sites in question to any parent corporation or entity.
   b. The overall financial resources of any parent corporation or entity.
   c. The overall size of the parent corporation or entity with respect to the number of employees.
   d. The number, type, and location of its facilities.
   e. The type of operation or operations of any parent corporation or entity, including the composition, structure, and functions of the work force of the parent corporation or entity.[10]

While these factors are vague, the DOJ gives some clarity in the regulations governing the removal of architectural barriers as to what may be readily achievable. Examples include:

- Installing ramps
- Making curb cuts in sidewalks and entrances
- Repositioning shelves
- Rearranging tables, chairs, vending machines, display racks, and other furniture
- Repositioning telephones
- Adding raised markings on elevator control buttons
- Installing flashing alarm lights
- Widening doors
- Eliminating a turnstile or providing an alternative accessible path
- Installing accessible door hardware
- Installing grab bars in toilet stalls
- Rearranging toilet partitions to increase maneuvering space
- Insulating lavatory pipes under sinks to prevent burns
- Installing a raised toilet seat
- Installing a full-length bathroom mirror
- Repositioning the paper towel dispenser in a bathroom
- Creating designated accessible parking spaces
- Installing an accessible paper cup dispenser at an existing inaccessible water fountain
- Removing high-pile, low-density carpeting
- Installing vehicle hand controls[11]

The DOJ also prioritizes the removal of architectural barriers as follows:

1. Provide access to a place of public accommodation from public sidewalks, parking, or public transportation.
2. Provide access to those areas of a place of public accommodation where goods and services are made available to the public.
3. Provide access to restroom facilities.
4. Take any other necessary measures to provide access to the goods, services, facilities, privileges, advantages, or accommodations of a place of public accommodation.[12]

"Undue burden" also plays a role in Title III analysis. A place of public accommodation must provide auxiliary aids and services unless to do so would constitute an undue burden or result in a fundamental alteration in the business.[13] To illustrate this principle, consider the following example:

> Every month the board of directors of a nonprofit social service agency meets. Persons with disabilities are very interested in attending, and they need various auxiliary aids and services in order to do so. What must the agency do?

Auxiliary aids and services include such varied items as:

- qualified interpreters, notetakers, computer-aided transcription services, written materials, telephone handset amplifiers, assistive listening devices, assistive listening systems, telephones compatible with hearing aids, closed-caption decoders, open and closed captioning, TTY machines, videotext displays, or other effective methods of making aurally delivered materials available to individuals with hearing impairments;
- qualified readers, taped texts, audio recordings, Brailled materials, large-print materials, or other effective methods of making visually delivered materials available to individuals with visual impairments;
- acquisition or modification of equipment or devices; and
- other similar services and actions.[14]

The same factors for determining whether the removal of barriers is readily achievable are also used by the DOJ to determine the existence of an undue burden.[15] The entity must provide the auxiliary aid or service unless to do so would fundamentally alter the business or jeopardize the entire entity's finances (with respect to the latter, the reader is again commended to *Olmstead v. L.C.*).

It's also possible that a person wanting to attend the board meeting may not need any auxiliary aid or service at all, but simply a change in the meeting time. This was precisely the case in *Dees v. Austin Travis County Mental Health and Mental Retardation*.[16] In *Dees*, a person with severe mental illness, who nevertheless was very active in the community as an advocate, brought suit on the grounds that the agency's 8:00 A.M. time for board meetings discriminated against her and others like her whose medication regimen did not permit them to be alert early in the morning.[17] The court was not persuaded that changing the time of the board meetings would be an undue burden or constitute a fundamental alteration in the nature of the agency's business.[18] While this was a Title II case, there is no reason to expect that the decision would not have equal applicability to the matter of board meetings of nonprofit entities subject to Title III of the ADA.

With respect to altering an existing facility, those alterations must be done in accordance with very specific architectural guidelines. The DOJ defines an alteration as any change to a business covered by Title III that affects or could affect the usability of the building or facility or any part of the building or facility—a very broad definition.[19] Further, if a portion of a facility containing a primary function is altered, then the path of travel to that portion of the facility must also be made readily accessible to persons with disabilities.[20] The DOJ defines primary function as a major activity for which the facility is intended, such as, for example, customer services lobby, the dining area of a cafeteria, meeting rooms in a conference center, offices, and other work areas in which the activities of the entity are performed.[21] Finally, it is extremely important to note that many states have their own accessibility rules, and often they are more strict than the federal guidelines. Accordingly, it is extremely important to be knowledgeable about state laws and regulations in matters of architectural accessibility.

While all of this is very detailed and can be difficult to understand, many architects are already familiar with these requirements. However, do not rely solely on an architect's assurances that the ADA is being complied with, as architectural firms have been sued directly by persons with disabilities for designing athletic facilities that were not in compliance with ADA architectural standards.[22] Certainly, this hypothetical architectural firm would be liable for malpractice, as architects are expected to know that new facilities must be designed in accordance with strict ADA construction standards.

Another question is whether the tenant or the landlord has the responsibility for making needed modifications. The DOJ makes it quite clear that both are jointly liable when a place of public accommodation is not accessible.[23] Further, the terms of a lease do not matter vis-à-vis the person aggrieved, though they will govern how the costs will be apportioned.[24] Thus, preventive law demands the existence of language in the lease governing the responsibilities of the landlord and tenant for compliance with the ADA.

NOTES

1. 42 U.S.C. § 12182(b)(2)(A)(iv).
2. 28 C.F.R. § 36.303(a).
3. 28 C.F.R. § 36.401.
4. 42 U.S.C. § 12182(a).
5. 42 U.S.C. § 12181(7), 28 C.F.R. § 36.104.
6. 42 U.S.C. § 12187.
7. 42 U.S.C. § 12181(7)(J).
8. 42 U.S.C. § 12181(7)(E).
9. 28 C.F.R. § 36.104.
10. *Id.*
11. 28 C.F.R. § 36.304(b).
12. 28 C.F.R. § 36.304(c).
13. 28 C.F.R. § 36.303(a).
14. 28 C.F.R. § 36.303.
15. 28 C.F.R. § 36.104.
16. Dees v. Austin Travis County Mental Health and Mental Retardation, 860 F. Supp. 1186 (W.D. Tex. 1994).
17. *Id.* at 1187.
18. *Id.* at 1190-91.
19. 28 C.F.R. § 36.402(b).
20. 28 C.F.R. § 36.403.
21. 28 C.F.R. § 403 (b).
22. *See, e.g.,* Johanson v. Huizenga Holdings, 963 F. Supp. 1175 (S.D. Fla. 1997).
23. 28 C.F.R. § 36.201(b).
24. *Id.*

The ADA and the Health-Care Provider

9

THE AMERICANS WITH DISABILITIES ACT and health care deserves a separate section of its own, as the jurisprudence in this area is evolving in a completely different direction than any reading of the ADA and its regulations would predict. With regard to employment, the cases, particularly with respect to HIV, make a distinction between medical personnel who do invasive procedures and those who do not. When the individual with the disability is the patient, the cases are more typical of what one would expect from studying the ADA laws and regulations. While the courts are very pro-employer when cases involve medical personnel who are HIV-positive and engaged in invasive procedures, they are pro-plaintiff when it comes to personnel who will not do invasive procedures or when it comes to HIV-infected patients. To understand how this distinction evolved, one must look at the doctrine of informed consent.

The doctrine of informed consent is a legal doctrine mandating that health-care providers reveal all the material facts necessary for a reasonable patient to make the decision whether to undergo surgery.[1] It certainly can be argued that a reasonable patient would want to know the surgeon's HIV status. On the other hand, a person who is HIV-positive could well have a disability under the ADA,[2] and therefore the HIV confidentiality laws must be considered.[3] To date, the courts are allowing broad latitude to the employer to deal with the HIV-positive health-care provider who performs or is involved in invasive surgery.[4] Virtually no latitude is being given to the health-care provider who refuses to care for a person with HIV.[5] Taking the doctrine of informed consent to its conclusion, some courts are imposing an obligation on the provider to disclose his or her HIV status,[6] even though HIV confidentiality laws would seem to suggest that the health-care provider would have some discretion in deciding whether to disclose his or her HIV status to others.

The other reason for the distinction is the ADA concept of direct threat—in particular, the factors that are used to determine when a direct threat exists. In *School Board of Nassau County, Florida v. Arline*, the U.S. Supreme Court held that whether a person is a direct threat and thereby not otherwise qualified depends upon evaluating:

- the nature of the risk (how the disease is transmitted);
- the duration of the risk (how long the carrier is infectious);
- the severity of the risk (the potential harm to third parties); and
- the probability the disease will be transmitted and cause varying degrees of harm.[7]

With regard to the HIV-positive health-care provider performing invasive procedures, the courts have been concentrating on the latter two factors. That is, the severity of the risk (extreme—death) and the uncertain, in their view, etiology of HIV. Of course, if a disease other than HIV were involved, those points might not be as significant.

A question also arises as to whether a physician with staff privileges at a hospital who suffers from discrimination based on a disability can sue that hospital for violating the ADA. There are two possible approaches. First, regardless of how the physician is classified, he may claim that the hospital exercises sufficient control over him so he would be deemed an employee per *Clackamas*, discussed earlier in this book.[8] The other possibility is a Title III suit. A Title III suit would essentially borrow from *PGA Tour v. Martin* by claiming that the hospital cannot deny the privileges it offers by discriminating on the basis of disability. This approach has been successful in some cases.[9]

Finally, the first edition of this book spent considerable time discussing medical schools and the person with a disability. Since the Association of Medical Schools (AAMS) in June 2005 published a booklet on the ADA and medical schools, the reader is referred to that publication for questions about medical schools and the ADA. Keep in mind that the publication is written by the AAMC and should not be a substitute for independent legal advice on the ADA. Nevertheless, the reader may want to start with that publication should he or she be faced with such a problem.

NOTES

1. The leading case on informed consent is *Canterbury v. Spence*, 464 F.2d 772 (D.C. Cir. 1972). Informed consent now exists in every state, though specific details of the doctrine may vary. Thus, the reader is encouraged to research his or her own applicable informed consent doctrine for specific answers. Nevertheless, the general principles of informed consent are the same in all jurisdictions.
2. *See* Bragdon v. Abbott, 524 U.S. 624 (1998).
3. Just about all states have laws protecting the confidentiality of HIV information. The specific laws vary in their provisions. Thus, the reader's particular state law should be consulted to see if and when the confidentiality provisions will be overridden in favor of a duty to warn per the doctrine of informed consent.
4. A hospital may reassign an HIV-positive surgical assistant without violating the Rehabilitation Act of 1973. *See* Bradley v. Univ. of Texas M.D. Anderson Cancer Center, 3 F.3d 922 (5th Cir. 1993); *see also* Bragdon v. Abbott, *supra* note 2.
5. *Bragdon, supra*; United States v. Morvant, 898 F. Supp. 1157 (E.D. La. 1995).
6. *See, e.g.,* Faya v. Almaraz, 620 A.2d 327 (Md. 1993). Please note, the states vary on the circumstances where such a cause of action would exist for failure to disclose HIV status. Thus, readers are advised to research their own state law before reaching any final conclusions.
7. School Board of Nassau County, Fla. v. Arline, 480 U.S. 273, 288 (1987).
8. *See* Clackamas Gastroenterology Assocs., P.C. v. Wells, 538 U.S. 440 (2003).
9. Mentkowitz v. Posttstown Mem'l Med. Center, 154 F.3d 113 (3d Cir. 1998).

The Interrelationship Between the ADA and Other Laws   **10**

ONE OF THE MOST DIFFICULT ASPECTS of dealing with the Americans with Disabilities Act is where it interrelates with other laws. This chapter will highlight some of the more common ways the ADA interacts with other laws and suggest ways such interactions may be effectively managed.

ADA AND COLLECTIVE BARGAINING

Consider this scenario:

> Person X has a disability recognized by the ADA. He is a union member. The collective bargaining agreement has seniority provisions. The agreement also has a provision allowing a person with a disability to override seniority rights, providing that person petitions the union. The union, it is important to point out, does not have to consent. Person X invokes this provision, but the union declines to exercise it. Because of his disability, Person X must transfer to a different job, since he cannot perform the essential functions of the job with or without reasonable ac-

commodations. However, without the protection offered by the disability provision contained in the collective bargaining agreement, he is subject to being bumped from that position by a more senior person. Person X sues both the employer and the union. What is the result?

The fact pattern described is actually found in *Eckles v. Consolidated Rail Corporation*.[1] The issue before the court, in this case the Seventh Circuit, was whether the ADA requires as a reasonable accommodation that a disabled individual be given special job placement and job protections even if to do so is in violation of a bona fide seniority system in place under a collective bargaining agreement.[2] In *Eckles*, the Seventh Circuit opted to preserve the sanctity of the collective bargaining agreement rather than hold that reasonable accommodation provisions of the ADA should somehow trump the workings of the agreement.[3] However, not all courts agreed with *Eckles*,[4] and thus, the U.S. Supreme Court stepped in to clarify this issue.

The Supreme Court entered the fray of reasonable accommodations and collective bargaining agreements in *U.S. Airways v. Barnett*.[5] In *U.S. Airways, Inc.*, the plaintiff injured his back while working in the cargo-handling position at U.S. Airways.[6] The plaintiff activated his seniority rights and transferred to a less physically demanding mailroom position.[7] In U.S. Airway's seniority system, the position he transferred to periodically became open to seniority-based employee bidding.[8] The plaintiff subsequently learned that at least two employees senior to him intended to bid for the job he had transferred into.[9] The plaintiff petitioned U.S. Airways for an exception to their seniority system so that he could be allowed to remain in that job.[10] Eventually U.S. Airways decided not to make the exception and the plaintiff lost the job.[11] This led to an ADA suit claiming that U.S. Airways should have reasonably accommodated him by allowing him to continue in that job despite the seniority provisions.[12]

The Court was faced with polar-opposite positions. On the one hand, the Court was asked by the plaintiff to say that seniority provisions should always be overridden when a person with a disability needs an accommodation.[13] On the other hand, the defendant, U.S. Airways, claimed that seniority should always override a person with a disability's request for a reasonable accommodation.[14] In striking the middle ground, the Court reasoned as follows. First, it said that case law has recognized the importance of seniority to employee-management relations.[15] Second, the Court noted that lower courts had unanimously found that collectively bargained seniority rights trump reasonable accommodations under a very similar law, the Rehabilitation Act of 1973.[16] Third, several U.S. Courts of Appeals had reached a similar conclusion with respect to seniority and the ADA.[17] Fourth, the Court was not persuaded that there should be any difference between a collectively bargained system and one, like U.S. Airways, that was a seniority system imposed by management, because the advantages and any attendant difficulties of a seniority system are not limited to collectively bargained systems.[18] The Court then went on to describe the important employee benefits offered by seniority-based systems.[19] Finally, the Court said that there was nothing in the ADA itself to suggest that Congress intended to undermine seniority systems when it came to a person with a disability asking for reasonable accommodations.[20]

The Court then proceeded to place the burden on the plaintiff to show special circumstances exist so that the seniority system could be overridden.[21] The Court noted two special circumstances that might occur. First, the employer, having retained the right to change a seniority system unilaterally, does so fairly often so as to give the employee the expectation that one more exception would not make a difference.[22] Second, the plaintiff might show that the seniority system was riddled with so many exceptions that another exception would not matter.[23] The Court went on to say that those two special circumstances were not meant to be exclusive;[24] however, these kinds of listings tend to take on a rigidity of their own in subsequent opinions.

Justice O'Connor in her concurring opinion took a slightly different view of when a seniority system could be overridden by a request for a reasonable accommodation. In her view, it would entirely depend upon whether the position was vacant or not.[25] If the position was vacant, then a reasonable accommodation for a person with a disability should be made.[26] If the position was not vacant, then no such reasonable accommodation was called for.[27] O'Connor's approach has the advantage of simplicity, but the law is, of course, the majority opinion.

There are other ways in which the ADA can affect the collective bargaining context. Two issues come to mind immediately. First, whether an ADA claim must be arbitrated where there is a mandatory arbitration agreement. Second, whether a mandatory arbitration agreement precludes an independent lawsuit by the EEOC. With respect to the first question, in *Wright v. Universal Maritime Service Corp.,* the U.S. Supreme Court held that there was no presumption of arbitrability with respect to ADA claims.[28] Further, while the ADA could be waived under an arbitration clause, such a waiver must be clear and unmistakable.[29]

With respect to the second question, the case of *EEOC v. Waffle House, Inc.*[30] is instructive. In *Waffle House,* Mr. Baker had signed a mandatory arbitration agreement with his employer, Waffle House.[31] After suffering a seizure at work, Mr. Baker was terminated.[32] Mr. Baker never activated the arbitration agreement, but he did file a timely claim with the EEOC.[33] When the EEOC's attempt to resolve the dispute failed, EEOC brought an enforcement action against Waffle House.[34] In holding that the EEOC had a full range of remedies available to it regardless of any arbitration agreement,[35] the Supreme Court reasoned as follows.

First, the Court said that the 1972 amendment to Title VII of the Civil Rights Act created a system where the EEOC had the primary burden of litigation.[36] Those same amendments authorized the courts to impose a full range of remedies, and nowhere do those amendments mention arbitration proceedings.[37] Second, the Court noted that in 1991 Congress amended Title VII, which included amending the ADA accordingly, to allow the recovery of compensatory and punitive damages by a complaining party, a term that included the EEOC.[38] Third, the 1991 amendments to Title VII contain no suggestion that an arbitration agreement between private parties changes in any way the EEOC's options or remedies available to it.[39] Fourth, the Court drew on basic contract law when it stated that the EEOC was not a party to any arbitration agreement and therefore could not be bound by that agreement.[40] Fifth, the Court noted that if the EEOC decides to file suit on behalf of a person, the EEOC is in complete control of that person's case.[41] In fact, the Court noted that the EEOC has its own right to vindicate the public interest and does not stand in the shoes of the person upon whose behalf the suit is brought.[42] Sixth, the Court reasoned that the statute granting power to the EEOC makes clear that it has the authority to evaluate the strength of the public interest at stake.[43] Finally, the pro-arbitration policies of the Federal Arbitration Act do not require an agency to relinquish its statutory authority if it has not agreed to do so.[44] In short, *Waffle House* stands for the proposition that while an employee may be bound by an arbitration agreement, the EEOC is certainly not.[45]

WORKER'S COMPENSATION

Employers traditionally engaged in two worker's compensation practices that are now forbidden under the ADA. First, employers often asked a prospective employee what his worker's compensation history was prior to any conditional job offer, as discussed much earlier in this book. This practice is now illegal under the ADA, as it violates the ADA's ban on preemployment medical inquiries.[46] Second, employers would—and many still do—insist on a full return to work after the employee suffered an on-the-job injury. An employer who continues this practice will lose an ADA lawsuit if the doctor does not grant a full return to work to the employee, because the only issue under the ADA is whether the employee can perform the essential functions of the job with or without reasonable accommodations.[47] The best way for an employer to avoid problems is to have the doctor evaluate whether the employee can perform the essential functions of the job with or without reasonable accommodations and for the employer to *not* insist on a full return to work. Finally, it is quite possible that the issue of mitigating measures will also have to be dealt with in this context.

INDIVIDUALS WITH DISABILITIES IN EDUCATION ACT

The Individuals with Disabilities in Education Act (IDEA) governs the special education universe. The ADA comes into play because the definitions of disability under the ADA are far broader than those contained in the IDEA regulations. Hence, a school district needs to consider that when a student is not eligible for special education services under IDEA, the student is not otherwise protected under ADA. If the student does have a disability according to the ADA, then the public school will have to modify its program to reasonably accommodate the student, even if that student is not eligible for special education services.[48]

FAMILY AND MEDICAL LEAVE ACT

It is impossible to practice in the area of the ADA without encountering the Family and Medical Leave Act (FMLA). The FMLA covers employers of fifty or more people[49] and permits an employee to take twelve weeks of leave (the leave could be paid or unpaid depending on whether the employer mandates the use of sick and vacation time first) to deal with his own or a family member's serious health condition.[50] Job protections are built into the legislation.[51] The scope of coverage of the FMLA and the ADA are very different. The ADA pertains to persons with disabilities, while the FMLA pertains to a serious health condition. The two are not the same. Nor does the term *serious health condition* mean what it appears to mean.[52] For example, one definition of a serious health condition is a period of incapacity of more than three days requiring continuing treatment from a physician.[53] That definition is extremely broad, much more so than any of the definitions of disability contained within the ADA.

The FMLA allows an employer to insist, providing there is a written policy, that an employee be certified as being eligible for leave or as being eligible to return to work from leave.[54] This creates a problem under the ADA, as the FMLA regulations stipulate that whether a person is eligible for FMLA or is allowed to return to work from the FMLA leave depends on whether the person can do the essential functions of the job.[55] Note that these regulations emphatically do not state that the certification must be based on whether the person can do the job *with or without reasonable accommodations*.[56] Thus, a trap for the unwary exists. For example, Person X is on FMLA leave and also has a disability. He desires to come back to work, so he is evaluated per written policy of his company. The doctor who examines X determines that he cannot do the essential functions of the job. The company denies the return to work. However, he can do the job with reasonable accommodations, perhaps with a short period of time off. In this scenario, the company has not violated the FMLA but has violated the ADA.[57] This problem can be solved by the company's evaluating the person based upon whether he can perform the essential functions of the job with reasonable accommodations.

Take another example. Person X has a disability. The company has the person evaluated, and it is determined that he cannot perform the essential functions of the job. Thus, under the FMLA, he is entitled to the leave. However, Person X can perform the essential functions of the job with reasonable accommodation. By not granting the leave, even though it is willing to make reasonable accommodations, the company could well be violating the FMLA, even though its actions would be consistent with the ADA. Two possible ways to defuse this problem come to mind: First, evaluate the person on whether he could do the essential functions of the job with reasonable accommodations. If so, make the accommodations. One has to assume that most people would rather work than go on leave, much of which may be unpaid.[58] Second, if the person still doesn't want to work but wants to go on leave, then the employer should offer whatever accommodations are necessary. If the person refuses the accommodations, case law, which is supported by the applicable regulations, for some time now has held that he is not protected by the ADA.[59] Even so, this person would still be entitled to leave under the FMLA.

ADA AND DISABILITY/ERISA BENEFITS

Consider the following scenario:

> Person X works for a company of over fifteen employees, develops a disability, and is terminated from her position because of that disability. She then files for Social Security benefits. Or perhaps she files for short-term or long-term disability benefits under the company's policy. She then brings suit under the ADA for failure of the employer to reasonably accommodate her disability.

The defense in this type of case is invariably based on the case of *Cleveland v. Policy Management Systems*,[60] where the person in some other proceeding has claimed total disability and is therefore estopped, or prevented, from claiming that he or she can do the job with or without reasonable accommodation. In *Cleveland* the plaintiff filed for Social Security Disability Benefits and obtained them.[61] Subsequently, he filed an ADA suit and claimed that he was not reasonably accommodated.[62] To obtain SSDI, a person has to show that he is unable to perform any job in the economic marketplace.[63]

In holding that judicial estoppel might apply in such situations, Justice Breyer, writing for the U.S. Supreme Court, wasted no time in laying out the holding of the case. Justice Breyer said that the pursuit and receipt of SSDI benefits do not automatically estop the plaintiff from pursuing an ADA claim.[64] Nor does the law erect a strong presumption against the plaintiff's success in filing an ADA claim.[65] However, an ADA plaintiff cannot simply ignore her SSDI contention.[66] To survive a motion for summary judgment, the plaintiff must explain why the information in the SSDI filing is consistent with showing that the plaintiff is otherwise qualified for the position at issue.[67]

Second, Justice Breyer took note of the apparent conflict between the ADA and SSDI, but proceeded to say the inherent conflict (the ADA saying, "I can do the job if I am reasonably accommodated" v. SSDI saying, "I can't do any job in the economic marketplace") was not so severe that courts should apply a special negative presumption.[68]

Third, the ADA and SSDI systems operate completely differently from each other. For example, the SSDI system does not factor reasonable accommodation into its calculus. Thus, an ADA suit claiming that the plaintiff can perform the job with reasonable accommodation may be consistent with claiming the inability to perform a job or jobs without it.[69]

Fourth, Justice Breyer noted that people receiving SSDI can work under certain parameters.[70]

Finally, even with all this said, an ADA plaintiff cannot ignore the SSDI and ADA apparent contradiction; a sufficient explanation must be forthcoming.[71] In order to defeat a summary judgment motion, the explanation must be sufficient to warrant a reasonable juror concluding that (assuming the truth of the claims made or the plaintiff's good-faith belief in the truth of those claims made in the SSDI filing), the plaintiff would nonetheless perform the essential functions of the job with or without reasonable accommodation.[72]

Thus, the Supreme Court has clarified just how judicial estoppel will be treated in the future vis-á-vis the ADA. What it means for the practitioner is that when filing an SSDI claim or a long-term disability claim on behalf of the client, *form* will become very important. That is, it will have to be made clear that the filing assumes that reasonable accommodations are a non-issue. Failure to take those precautions could well sink the client later if he or she pursues an ADA claim. Also, it is no longer SSDI that is the sole worry, as courts are now holding that representations made in a long-term disability application may also activate judicial estoppel.[73] Finally, the practitioner of the ADA and the practitioner of SSDI must let the client know of the risks of judicial estoppel when taking on their ADA or SSDI matter. A lawyer who fails to so advise the client runs the real risk of legal malpractice.[74]

NOTES

1. Eckles v. Consol. Rail Corp., 94 F.3d 1041, 1043-44 (7th Cir. 1996).
2. *Id.* at 1045.
3. *Id.* at 1051.
4. *See* Aka v. Washington Hosp. Center, 156 F.3d 1284, 1303 (D.C. Cir. 1998).
5. U.S. Airways, Inc. v. Barnett, 535 U.S. 391 (2002).
6. *Id.* at 394.
7. *Id.*
8. *Id.*
9. *Id.*
10. *Id.*
11. *Id.*
12. *Id.*
13. *Id.* at 396.
14. *Id.*
15. *Id.* at 403.
16. *Id.*
17. *Id.*
18. *Id.* at 404.
19. *Id.*
20. *Id.* at 405.
21. *Id.*
22. *Id.*
23. *Id.*
24. *Id.*
25. *Id.* at 408-10 (O'Connor, J., concurring).
26. *Id.* at 409-10. (O'Connor. J., concurring).
27. *Id.*
28. Wright v. Universal Maritime Serv. Corp., 525 U.S. 70, 79 (1998).
29. *Id.* at 80.
30. E.E.O.C. v. Waffle House, Inc., 534 U.S. 279 (2002).
31. *Id.* at 282-83.

32. *Id.* at 283.
33. *Id.*
34. *Id.*
35. *Id.* at 298.
36. *Id.* at 286.
37. *Id.*
38. *Id.* at 287.
39. *Id.* at 288.
40. *Id.* at 289-90.
41. *Id.* at 291-92.
42. *Id.* at 297.
43. *Id.* at 291.
44. *Id.* at 294.
45. *Id.* at 297.
46. *See* EEOC Enforcement Guidance: Worker's Compensation and the ADA, September 1996.
47. *See* EEOC Enforcement Guidance on Disability-Related Inquiries and Medical Examinations of Employees under the ADA, July 2000.
48. *See* William D. Goren, *IDEA, Its Interrelationship to the ADA & Preventive Law*, 71 Fla B. J. 76 (1997).
49. 29 U.S.C. § 2611(4)(A)(1).
50. 29 U.S.C. § 2612(a).
51. 29 U.S.C. § 2614; *see also* 29 C.F.R. § 825.214.
52. 29 C.F.R. § 825.114.
53. 29 C.F.R. § 825.114(a)(2)(i).
54. 29 U.S.C. § 2613; *see also* 29 C.F.R. § 825.310.
55. 29 C.F.R. § 825.115.
56. *Id.*
57. *See* EEOC Enforcement Guidance on Reasonable Accommodations and Undue Hardship Under the Americans With Disabilities Act at #21 (October 2002).
58. *See id.*; 29 C.F.R. § 825.207.
59. *See* 29 C.F.R. 1630.9(d), which explicitly states that a person rejecting a reasonable accommodation disqualifies him or herself from ADA protections.
60. *See generally* Cleveland v. Policy Mgmt. Sys. Corp., 526 U.S. 795 (1999).
61. *Id.* at 798-99.
62. *Id.* at 799.
63. *Id.* at 973-74.
64. *Id.* at 802-03.
65. *Id.* at 802.
66. *Id.* at 806.
67. *Id.* at 806-07.
68. *Id.* at 802-03.
69. *Id.* at 803.

70. *Id.* at 805.
71. *Id.* at 805-07.
72. *Id.* at 807.
73. *See* Opsteen v. Keller Structures, Inc., 408 F.3d 390 (7th Cir. 2005).
74. *See generally* William D. Goren, The Intersection of the ADA and SSDI and the Risks of Legal Malpractice, DCBA Brief, http://www.dcba.org/brief/marissue/2006/art10306.htm

Remedies and Procedural Issues

11

WHAT ARE THE REMEDIES OFFERED BY THE ADA? Each title offers different remedies, and they deserve separate treatment. Title I remedies are keyed into the Civil Rights Act of 1964, including the exhaustion of remedies requirement.[1] Prior to filing a lawsuit, a person alleging discrimination in employment based on disability must first exhaust the EEOC process and receive a right-to-sue letter. The EEOC has streamlined its procedures for processing complaints, and one should be able to procure a right-to-sue letter earlier than in the past. Once the EEOC process has been completed, a claim can be filed in court. If intentional discrimination can be proven, the remedies available under the Civil Rights Act of 1964, which include compensatory and punitive damages, can be obtained. However, if the issue of reasonable accommodations is involved, the employer can prevent an award of damages if it can show that it made a good-faith effort to accommodate the person with a disability.[2] The compensatory and punitive damages for violating the ADA can be very steep, and the maximum amount of damages available depends upon how many employees an employer has in each of twenty or more calendar weeks in the current or preceding calendar year. The range is as follows:

- 15–100 workers: $50,000
- 101–200 workers: $100,000
- 201–500 workers: $200,000
- 501 or more workers: $300,000[3]

The ADA is one of those statutes that allows for recovery of attorney fees should the plaintiff prevail.[4] The question is, what does it mean to prevail? A case that addressed that issue is *Buckhannon Board and Care Home, Inc. v. West Virginia Department of Health and Human Resources.*[5] In *Buckhannon*, an operator of group homes for persons with disabilities failed an inspection by the fire marshal's office because the residents were not capable of self-preservation.[6] When it received orders to close the facility, it sued, alleging violations of the Fair Housing Act and the ADA.[7] Subsequent to the suit, the state legislature eliminated the self-preservation requirement.[8] Buckhannon then brought a claim for attorney's fees claiming that the lawsuit brought about a desired voluntary change in the defendant's conduct (commonly referred to as the catalyst theory).[9] Since not all of the U.S. Courts of Appeals agreed with the catalyst theory, the Supreme Court took the case to resolve the conflict.[10] In rejecting the catalyst theory, the U.S. Supreme Court reasoned as follows. First, the Court, as it often does, referred to a dictionary (in this case *Black's Law Dictionary*) definition of the term *prevailing*, which refers to a judgment or some relief being given by the court.[11] Second, the Court looked to its prior case law to find it had declared that Congress had intended, with respect to other civil rights fee-shifting provisions, that the plaintiff receive at least some relief on the merits of the claim, even if the relief is nominal, before it can be said the plaintiff has prevailed.[12] Third, the Court noted that it had previously said that private settlements enforced through a consent decree also result in a party being considered to have prevailed.[13] Fourth, the Court noted that the legislative history of the Civil Rights Attorneys Fees Award Act was ambiguous as to whether Congress intended for the catalyst theory to apply, and absent clear legislative intent to the contrary, the Court was unwilling to part with the American rule (which holds that each party to a suit is responsible for its own attorney's fees).[14] Finally, the Court was concerned that adopting the catalyst theory would lead to another set of full-blown litigation to determine why the defendant changed its conduct.[15]

What *Buckhannon* means for the practitioner is that he or she should probably avoid linking any fee to an award of attorneys' fees, if indeed the practitioner does this in the first place, and allow himself the flexibility of collecting under his other rate, oftentimes contingency on the plaintiff's side, should an attorney fees award not be in the cards. After all, most suits settle privately without any judicial oversight. Alternatively, the plaintiff's lawyer desirous of obtaining an attorney's fee award should see if there is not some way he or she can get the court involved in the settlement process and its oversight, such as a consent decree, for example. Of course, on the defense side, the attorneys would want to settle privately without any future judicial oversight or any kind of decision on the merits.

Remedies under Title II of the ADA are linked to the Rehabilitation Act of 1973.[16] Accordingly, courts have held that a person alleging violation of Title II does not have to exhaust administrative remedies prior to bringing suit.[17]

Title II of the ADA requires that governmental entities of fifty or more people have a grievance procedure for ADA complaints.[18] This requirement raises a legitimate question as to whether a person suing under Title II of the ADA must first exhaust the public entity's internal ADA grievance procedure. While the Department of Justice says exhaustion of the internal grievance procedure would not be required,[19] one could present arguments in favor of it. Clearly, the court system is already clogged, and exhausting the grievance procedure offers an opportunity to communicate the problem to the employer and resolve it before a court fight. Undertaking the grievance procedure and handling it effectively would also allow the governmental entity to demonstrate good faith in trying to resolve the claim. Then, too, a person with a disability has an issue that needs to be respected, and airing the grievance internally often can resolve the entire dispute. Finally, equity would seem to demand that the governmental entity be given a chance to resolve the issue before becoming embroiled in litigation. Regardless of any legal requirement to exhaust internal remedies first, good preventive lawyering would suggest that governmental entities, regardless of size, have an ADA grievance procedure, and that the plaintiff might want to consider exhausting that procedure first before filing suit under the ADA so as to avoid expensive litigation.

Title III of the ADA operates quite differently from the other two titles. For instance, administrative remedies do not have to be exhausted,[20] and the only remedy available for a person who brings a private cause of action is injunctive relief and lawyers' fees.[21] The regulatory agency for Title III of the ADA—as well as Title II, for that matter—is the Department of Justice, and it can fine violators up to $50,000 for a first violation and up to $100,000 for each subsequent violation.[22] No punitive damages are available.[23] With the remedies being so limited under Title III, there have nevertheless been some surprising developments. First, despite the limited remedies, many Title III suits have been filed. Second, the Department of Justice has very actively pursued violations of Title III, and that has led to Title III violators paying fines and damages to the aggrieved plaintiff.

To recover under the ADA, does a plaintiff have to prove that the discrimination he or she suffered was solely because of the disability? What *does* a plaintiff have to prove in order to recover under the ADA? With respect to the first question, over the last six years since the first edition was published, the law has settled somewhat in this area. That is, it now seems clear that what has to be shown is not sole cause but whether the disability made a difference in the outcome of the adverse decision.[24]

Turning to the area of the burdens of proof, it varies depending upon whether disparate impact or disparate treatment is involved. Both theories are available to a plaintiff alleging violation of the ADA.[25] That said, the two theories differ from each other. With disparate impact, you have a facially neutral policy that adversely impacts, in this case, persons with disabilities.[26] In a disparate impact case, it is possible for a facially neutral employment practice to be found discriminatory without evidence of the employer's subjective intent to discriminate against a class of people.[27] A disparate treatment case is different. In a disparate treatment case, the employer treats some people less favorably than others because of their protected characteristic.[28] Whether a person is liable for disparate treatment depends upon whether the protected trait actually motivated the employer's decision.[29] In a disparate treatment case, the plaintiff must first make a prima facie case that he or she was discriminated against.[30] Once the plaintiff accomplishes this, it is up to the employer to offer a nondiscriminatory reason for the adverse employment action.[31] If the employer does so, then the plaintiff is given the opportunity to prove that it was more likely than not that the reasons given by the employer were really a pretext for discrimination.[32]

In a Title II case, a plaintiff has to show proof that is similar to that shown in a Title I case. In order to recover, the plaintiff must show that (1) he or she is a qualified individual with a disability; (2) he or she was excluded from participation in or denied the benefits of some public entity's services, programs, or activities; and (3) the discrimination suffered was because of the disability.[33]

Finally, if a Title III case is involved, a plaintiff has to show that (1) he or she is within the protected class of persons with disabilities; (2) the defendants are owners or operators of a place of public accommodation; and (3) the defendants discriminated against the plaintiff by denying him or her a full and equal opportunity to participate in or benefit from the defendants' program because of the disability.[34]

VOIR DIRE

Can a lawyer use peremptory challenges to discriminate against prospective jurors with disabilities? The question is not as far-fetched as one would think. In California, a state prosecutor used peremptory challenges to dismiss obese women from the jury. When asked why, he said he did not like obese women. How would such exclusions play out under *Batson* and its civil progeny, *Edmonson*?[35]

A "*Batson* challenge" is named for *Batson v. Kentucky*, in which the U.S. Supreme Court held that peremptory challenges could not be used to discriminate racially in criminal proceedings without violating the Equal Protection Clause of the Fifth Amendment.[36] This prohibition was extended to civil proceedings in *Edmonson v. Leesville Concrete Company* and to gender in *J.E.B. v. Alabama* ex rel. *T.B.*[37] A lawyer will exercise a *Batson* challenge if he or she believes that the other side is using peremptories to strike persons on the basis of a protected characteristic.[38] Once the lawyer is able to make a prima facie showing that the jury is being selected in that way, the burden shifts to the other lawyer to give a reasonable explanation for the exclusion.[39] The judge, of course, makes the final call.[40] Would *Batson* and its progenies apply to persons with disabilities? In the first edition of the book, I posited that the policy behind the *Batson* decision and its civil progeny applied with equal force to persons with disabilities. Subsequent to that edition, the Seventh Circuit in *United States v. Har-*

ris held that *Batson* did not apply to persons with disabilities.[41] However, there can be little doubt that under the Supreme Court case of *Lane v. Tennessee*, *Batson* applies to persons with disabilities.

In *Lane*, the Court listed a variety of basic constitutional guarantees subject to a more searching review than rational basis.[42] That list included according the civil litigant the meaningful opportunity to be heard by removing obstacles to full participation in judicial proceedings and ensuring that the criminal defendant gets the right to trial by jury from a fair cross-section of the community.[43] The Court, in listing various cases where people were discriminated against on the basis of their disabilities by states in the non-employment context included a case involving a deaf person excluded from jury service and a case where a peremptory challenge was used to strike a hearing-impaired juror.[44] Thus, there can be little doubt that *Batson* and its civil progeny apply to persons with disabilities.

NOTES

1. 42 U.S.C. § 12117(a).
2. 42 U.S.C. § 1977A(a)(3). *See also* EEOC v. Sears, *supra*.
3. 42 U.S.C. § 1977A(b).
4. Buckhannon Board and Care Home, Inc. v. W.Va. Dep't of Health and Human Resources, 532 U.S. 598, 602 (citing to 42 U.S.C. § 12205).
5. *See generally id.*
6. *Id.* at 600.
7. *Id.* at 600-01.
8. *Id.* at 601.
9. *Id.*
10. *Id.* at 602.
11. *Id.* at 603.
12. *Id.* at 603-04.
13. *Id.* at 604.
14. *Id.* at 607.
15. *Id.* at 608-09.
16. 42 U.S.C. § 12133.
17. *See* Doe v. County of Milwaukee, 871 F. Supp. 1072, 1076 (E.D. Wis. 1995).
18. 28 C.F.R. § 35.107(a).
19. 56 Fed. Reg. 35,694 (July 26, 1991) at discussion of 28 C.F.R. § 35.170.
20. 28 C.F.R. § 36.501.
21. *Id.*
22. 28 C.F.R. § 36.504(a)(3).

23. 28 C.F.R. § 36.504(c).
24. McNely v. Ocala Star-Banner Corp., 99 F.3d 1068, 1073-77 (1996).
25. Raytheon Co. v. Hernandez, 540 U.S. 44, 53 (2003).
26. *Id.* at 52.
27. *Id.* at 52-53.
28. *Id.* at 52.
29. *Id.*
30. *Id.* at 55.
31. *Id.*
32. *Id.* at 52.
33. Melton v. Dallas Area Rapid Transit, 391 F.3d 669, 671 (5th Cir. 2004).
34. Louie v. NFL, 185 F. Supp. 2d 1306, 1308 (S.D. Fla. 2002).
35. Batson v. Kentucky, 476 U.S. 79 (1986); Edmonson v. Leesville Concrete, 500 U.S. 614 (1991).
36. *Batson,* 476 U.S. at 84.
37. J.E.B. v. Alabama *ex rel.* T.B., 511 U.S. 127 (1994).
38. *Batson, supra*, 476 U.S. at 93-94.
39. *Id.* at 94-97.
40. *Id.* at 98.
41. United States v. Harris, 197 F.3d 870 (7th Cir. 1999).
42. *Lane,* 541 U.S. at 523.
43. *Id.*
44. *Id.* at 525 n.14.

ADA and Sports 12

PROFESSIONAL SPORTS

THE AREA OF PROFESSIONAL SPORTS and the Americans with Disabilities Act is a topic that bears exploring. This hypothetical is based on a real-life occurrence:

> A professional basketball player develops an irregular heartbeat. The team sends the player for tests and refuses to let him play in the meantime. Six weeks of tests are inconclusive. Further, the NBA's insurance company will not insure the ballplayer. The player also interviews with other teams and takes their physical as a condition of the team pursuing further interest in him. There is no interest there. Finally, the team the player played for in the past tenders him a one-year offer but refuses to let him play unless he takes a genetic test that might reveal whether he has some genetic abnormality that would put him at risk in the future. The basketball player refuses to take the test. Any ADA issues?[1]

Title I of the ADA governs this scenario because an employment relationship is involved. Since there is no exemption for professional sports anywhere in the ADA, and all professional sports teams have at least fifteen employees, Title I of the ADA applies here and to the operations of professional sports teams in general.

This hypothetical case raises several ADA issues, including:

- preemployment and post-employment medical exams;
- job-relatedness, business necessity, and whether the person can perform the job with reasonable accommodations;
- the definition of disability;
- essential functions of the job of a pro athlete or coach/manager; and
- defenses that the team may have when an ADA claim is filed.

Turning to the first set of issues, did the other team's interest in our pro basketball player violate the ADA's prohibition on preemployment medical exams? Whether an illegal preemployment medical exam has occurred is an issue that operates independently of whether the employee has a disability under the ADA.[2] The preemployment medical exam issue will arise whenever a player is traded or signs on as a free agent. As noted earlier, the ADA prohibits preemployment medical exams.[3] A medical exam (any exam that solicits information about a person's health or possible disability) can take place *after* a conditional job offer is made.[4] A conditional job offer can be withdrawn if it is job-related, consistent with business necessity, and the person could not do the essential functions of the job with or without reasonable accommodations.[5] When a player is traded contingent on passing a physical, does a preemployment medical exam occur or is the medical exam conducted after a conditional job offer? Clearly, the player has not yet been employed by the team trading for him. On the other hand, the team will hire the player if he can pass the physical. Therefore, it can be argued that these physicals are done pursuant to a conditional job offer and that no illegal preemployment medical exam occurs. Still, the issue of whether a preemployment medical exam occurred is very significant because if it did, the ADA was violated. If the exam was made pursuant to a conditional job offer, further analysis under the ADA is needed.

Assume for the sake of argument that these physicals of pro players are done after a conditional job offer. Let's further assume that, based on our player's heart condition, the team withdraws the offer to our player. Therefore, the question becomes whether the job offer was withdrawn for reasons related to the job, consistent with business necessity, and where the person was unable to perform the essential functions of the job with reasonable accommodations. Again, all three requirements must be satisfied before a conditional job offer can be validly withdrawn. Certainly, whenever a player is traded or signed and a physical is performed, it is certainly job-related and consistent with business necessity. However, if an offer were to be withdrawn after the physical, could the team show that the athlete could not perform the essential functions of the job with or without reasonable accommodations? The first step is to determine the essential functions of the employee's job. In determining the essential functions of the job of an NBA player, for example, the potential exists for confusing tasks with functions. For example, it could be said that jumping, stopping, and running are all tasks associated with the job of the pro basketball player. It also could be said that rebounding, shooting, and playing defense are essential functions of the job. When it comes to determining essential functions of the job, preventive law demands that functions are relevant and tasks are not. For example, shooting, rebounding, and playing defense are *functions* of playing basketball, whereas jumping, running, and stopping are the *tasks* that are used to perform those functions. The reason for the distinction is that people use various means to accomplish the same function, and nowhere is that more clear than on the hardwood. For example, Dennis Rodman (6'9") used his jumping and blocking-out abilities to rebound, while a player well over seven feet—and there are quite a few of them in the NBA—doesn't have to jump at all.

Did the team even have the right to insist on a post-employment medical exam? The answer is yes, because a post-employment medical exam, as we have already discussed, can be done where it is job-related and consistent with business necessity.[6] Certainly, the ability of our player to survive the rigors of an NBA game is related to his job. Also, considering all the dollars the team has potentially wrapped up in this player, it is certainly consistent with business necessity to have the tests done.

The question then becomes what the team does with the results of the testing. Let's say the tests are inconclusive and the player wants to play. The team is scared of the possibilities, especially since it can't get insurance on the player. The team refuses to let the player play. Does the team have any available defenses when an ADA suit is brought against it by an athlete or athletic personnel? Four defenses immediately come to mind: First, the team may allege that the disability is only temporary. Second, the team may allege that the player is a direct threat to himself or others. In the right case,[7] direct threat could be an excellent defense. Third, a team may claim that the player does not have a disability under the ADA. More specifically, the team might claim that the player is not substantially limited in any major life activity and is therefore not a person with a disability under the ADA, even though he may have a physical impairment.[8] Such a defense has a strong chance of succeeding, especially in light of one logical reading of *Sutton v. United Airlines* when read in conjunction with *Toyota Motor*, both of which we have previously discussed. Fourth, as mentioned in Chapter 3, an employer is not required to make accommodations for a person if doing so means that its business would be fundamentally altered. For example, if a player were suing for lack of playing time based on a perceived disability, this defense could be used.

Let's return now to our basketball player. Does our player have a physical or mental impairment that substantially limits a major life activity? Certainly, the physical or mental impairment, irregular heartbeat, is present, but what about the substantial limitation on major life activity? Newspaper reports said that nobody could figure out what was wrong. Also, is our pro basketball player severely restricted or prevented from performing a major life activity, under one possible reading of *Toyota Motor*? Is he even limited in a substantial major life activity when compared to the average person per the analysis of *EEOC v. Sears*, also discussed earlier in this book? We really don't have enough facts. However, on these limited facts, it would seem hard to believe that our pro basketball player could have a disability under the ADA.

Let's assume for the sake of argument that somehow our pro basketball player did have a disability or was perceived as having a disability. Might the team argue that the pro basketball player was a direct threat to himself per *Chevron*?[9] For this defense to succeed, it would have to be based on the best available scientific evidence or the best objective evidence.[10] Answering this question would mean scouring the medical records and then hiring medical experts to reach a conclusion as to whether he would be a direct threat. In short, a direct threat defense would be very expensive for the team in this case. Even so, considering the stakes involved, mounting a direct threat defense might be worth the money. In any event, regardless of the outlay of any monies to prove direct threat, the player will still have an extremely difficult threshold issue to get over vis-á-vis whether the ADA would even consider him disabled.

A discussion of the ADA and professional sports cannot be complete without a discussion of the Supreme Court case of *PGA Tour, Inc. v. Martin.*[11] In *PGA Tour,* Casey Martin, a teammate of Tiger Woods at Stanford, filed for permission to use a cart at the third stage of "Q" school.[12] Q school is one of the ways that a golfer can qualify to play on the Nike or PGA Tours (the Nike tour being one step below the PGA Tour).[13] During the first two stages of Q school, carts are permitted.[14] However, carts are not permitted at the last stage.[15] Martin suffered from Klippel-Trenaunay-Weber Syndrome, a degenerative circulatory disorder that obstructs the flow of blood from his right leg back to his heart.[16] The disease is progressive and causes severe pain and atrophies the right leg.[17] In college, he reached a point where he could no longer walk an 18-hole golf course.[18] Thus, he successfully petitioned the NCAA for the right to use a cart.[19] When he turned pro and successfully completed the first two rounds of Q school, he petitioned the PGA for the right to use a cart and attached extensive medical records.[20] The PGA Tour refused to review the records and denied his request to use a cart.[21] It should be noted that while the Ninth Circuit agreed with Martin, the Seventh Circuit in a virtually identical case held for the golf tour.[22] Thus, it was up to the Supreme Court to resolve the conflict among the Circuits.

The Supreme Court had two issues before it: first, whether the PGA was even subject to the ADA,[23] and second, if the PGA was subject to the ADA, whether Martin's request to use a cart was a reasonable accommodation.[24] Since all parties agreed that Martin was a person with a disability, the issue of whether Martin had a disability was not before the Court.[25] Turning to the first issue, the Court held that the PGA was subject to the ADA vis-á-vis people trying to qualify for its tour and not just people who might watch tour events.[26] In reaching this conclusion, the Court reasoned as follows. First, Title III of the ADA prohibits discrimination against persons with disabilities in the full and equal enjoyment of the goods, services, facilities, privileges, advantages, or accommodations of any place of public accommodation by any person owning, leasing, or operating a place of public accommodation.[27] Second, the Court noted that golf courses were explicitly mentioned in the definition of what is a public accommodation.[28] Third, the Court referred to the language that a lessee could not discriminate against a person with a disability (the PGA Tour being such a lessee for its events).[29] Fourth, the Court said that one of the privileges offered by this lessee is the chance to play on its tours depending on how well the person does in Q school.[30] Thus, the PGA Tour simply could not under the ADA deny a person equal access to its tours on the basis of disability.[31] The PGA attempted to persuade the Court that different rules applied depending upon whether one was a spectator or a competitor.[32] The Court simply did not buy the argument.[33] The Court believed that watching the tour and competing in the tour were two separate privileges offered by the PGA, both of which had to be accessible to persons with disabilities.[34] To hold otherwise, the Court felt, would be inconsistent with the literal text of the ADA itself as well as with its expansive purpose to read the provisions of Title III broadly.[35]

The second issue the Court was faced with was whether granting Martin's use of the cart would fundamentally alter the nature of the game of golf. In holding that such an accommodation would have no such result and therefore was reasonable, the Court reasoned as follows. First, the Court began by observing that the fundamental character of the game of golf was shot-making.[36] Second, the Court noted that golf has evolved over the years to include golf bags, caddies, carts pulled by hand, and motorized carts that carry players as well clubs.[37] The Court went on to note that motorized cars are often encouraged because they speed up play and are a moneymaker.[38] Third, the Court noted that nothing in the rules of golf either prevents the use of a cart or penalizes players for using it.[39] In fact, whether a golfer uses a cart does not even factor into the golfer's handicap.[40] Fourth, the walking rule cited by the PGA was actually not a rule of golf but buried as an optional condition in the appendix to the rules of golf.[41] Fifth, the Court stated that the walking rule was not an indispensable feature of tournament golf, either.[42] The Court noted that the PGA permits golf carts to be used in the Senior PGA Tour, the open qualifying event for PGA tournaments, the Senior Men and Women's Amateur championships, the first two stages of Q school, and until 1997, the third stage of Q school as well.[43] Sixth, the Court said that pure chance may have a greater impact on the outcome of elite golf tournaments than the fatigue resulting from the enforcement of the walking rule.[44] Seventh, the Court noted that the district court had found that the fatigue from walking during a tournament was not significant and that any fatigue incurred by the golfer was the result of psychological factors, such as stress and motivation.[45] Further, even if the rule did promote fatigue, the district court found that Casey Martin, even with a cart, endured more fatigue than the average golfer.[46] Eighth, the Court stated that the ADA makes no exception for elite athletics.[47] Ninth, the Court said that the PGA erred in not making an individual inquiry as to whether the requested accommodation would fundamentally alter the nature of the game.[48]

If anything can be taken away from *PGA Tour*, it is that the ADA applies to elite athletics. Thus, the practitioner needs to keep in mind that even elite athletes may, under certain circumstances, come under the ambit of the ADA.

ADA AND COLLEGE OR HIGH SCHOOL SPORTS

Applying the ADA to college or high school sports raises a completely different set of issues. Assuming the high school or college is a public entity, its programs and activities must be accessible in order to comply with Title II of the ADA. Consider the college or high school wheelchair athlete who wants to run track and play tennis. Is the track program or tennis accessible to the person in the wheelchair? In *Hollenbeck v. Board of Education of Rochelle Township*,[49] a school denied a student's request to participate in track and tennis, and the student brought suit under the Individuals with Disabilities Education Act (IDEA). In the due process hearing held pursuant to the requirements of that act, the hearing officer found for the student and ordered the school to assess in which sports the student could participate.[50] The school district did not obey the hearing officer's guidelines, and the student once again brought suit.[51] The court held that the board failed to observe its obligations set forth in the hearing officer's decision.[52] Further, the court held that the student was not evaluated properly. In fact, there was no medical evaluation at all. Nor was the multidisciplinary team formed in such a way that a fair assessment could be made, as none of the multidisciplinary team members had any expertise with mobility-impaired athletes.[53] In short, the court found that Hollenbeck's civil rights had been violated by the school.[54]

While this case involved IDEA, there would be many similar things to consider if this were an ADA claim. For example, the student would have to be carefully evaluated, and people knowledgeable about wheelchair athletics would have to be involved in the assessment. The issue of whether the student would be a danger to others while competing would also have to be considered. Finally, the program would have to be modified, unless to do so would constitute an undue burden or fundamentally alter the program. It is unlikely that the money involved in making an accommodation would be a good defense, so the issue of whether the program would be fundamentally altered would have to be thoroughly and objectively analyzed.

The *Hollenbeck* case has an interesting postscript. Hollenbeck took advantage of this case and competed successfully in track and field. He has competed in the U.S. Paralympics in Atlanta and has been seen in TV commercials for Nike.

All this is fine, but what if the college or university takes action against an athlete or refuses to accommodate an athlete because the NCAA rules leave it no choice, even though the athlete has a disability under the ADA? It's now pretty clear that the NCAA can be sued for violating the ADA under Title III of the ADA. Borrowing on cases such as *Weyer v. Twentieth Century Fox Film Corp.*, previously discussed in this book, courts have held that the NCAA exercises sufficient control over the athletic programs at member institutions so that one could say that a nexus exists between the entity covered by the ADA and the NCAA itself.[55]

ADA AND THE REFEREE

A discussion of the ADA and sports is not complete without a discussion of the people who ensure that a game is played fairly—the referees or umpires. Consider these facts:

A referee of college football games gains a great deal of weight. As a result, his performance declines. Eventually, he is told to lose weight or he will lose his job. He does not lose the weight, his performance continues to decline, and he is rated last in the conference. He is then terminated. He brings suit under the ADA. How might a court go about analyzing this case?

The first question is who does the referee sue, and under what title of the ADA? Many referees are independent contractors. Consequently, Title I of the ADA, which governs employment, may not apply. However, some referee associations exercise sufficient control over their referee members to justify the existence of an employer-employee relationship. If sufficient control does exist, the question becomes whether the referee association has at least fifteen employees. The referee may well find that many such associations do not, unless a court were to find that each referee in the association is an employee. This leaves the referee with Titles II and III from which to choose. The problem with utilizing Title II of the ADA is that a governmental entity may not be involved. After all, it is the conference or the referee association that informs the referee that he can no longer work, not a governmental entity. There is a possibility that the referee might be able to sue under Title II of the ADA through a roundabout way. That is, Title II prohibits governmental entities from contracting with any organization that discriminates on the basis of disability.[56] If the referee organization is discriminating on the basis of disability and it has a contract with a governmental entity, then the governmental entity could potentially be exposed to an ADA suit.

The referee could consider suing under Title III of the ADA. However, the problem he faces is that while places of recreation are places of public accommodation under the ADA,[57] it is not the place of recreation itself that is the problem. Rather, it is the ability of the person to referee a game in that place of recreation. For this theory, the referee might draw on *PGA Tour v. Martin*, discussed previously in this book, which said, among other things, that competitors at a place of public accommodation were subject to the ADA.[58] The referee may also look to the line of cases that will find a claim where a nexus exists between the site complained of and a place of public accommodation.[59] Regardless of the difficulty of finding the proper person to sue, assume for the sake of argument that a proper person to sue can be found. Then the question becomes whether the referee has a disability—that is, does he have a physical or mental impairment that substantially limits one or more of life's major activities? Morbid obesity, 100 percent above recommended weight, has been held to be a disability.[60] If the person is not morbidly obese, there may or may not be a physical impairment, but the person could still be perceived to have a disability.[61] The problem for the referee will be showing what major life activity is substantially limited by his weight and whether, depending on the Circuit, he is substantially limited at all.

If it can be shown that a major life activity is substantially limited, the next question is, can he perform the essential functions of the job with or without reasonable accommodations—that is, is he otherwise qualified? To determine this answer, the essential functions of a referee's job must be identified. On a basic level, an essential function of the job is to call the game accurately. Obesity certainly limits a referee's movement. If his obesity limits the referee's movement to the point where he can no longer get in the proper position in time to make a call, then he is not able to perform an essential job function. Finally, it is hard to envision what reasonable accommodations could be offered to a referee who, because of his disability, cannot make calls. Clearly, having other referees do his part of the job is not an option.

To summarize, the referee might find it difficult to sue the proper person. Even so, look for more cases in this area, because many referee associations fail to grasp that disability discrimination rules could possibly apply to their operations.

NOTES

1. This hypothetical is taken from media reports of the situation involving the Chicago Bulls and their center, Eddy Curry. Keep in mind that media reports are not always accurate. Thus, there may be many more critical details that we don't know. Nevertheless, I use this scenario as a way of illustrating various legal principles pertaining to the ADA. The matter has a happy ending for now. Eddy Curry was traded to the Knicks for some players and draft choices. He underwent extensive testing in New York and had those tests reviewed by Knick doctors and a doctor from the NBA, all of whom cleared him to play. *The New York Times* reports that the Knicks now have a very strong front court going into the 2005-06 season.
2. 42 U.S.C. § 12112(d)(2)(A). The reader is also referred to the discussion on preemployment medical exams that appeared earlier in this book.
3. 42 U.S.C. § 12112(d)(2)(A).

4. 42 U.S.C. § 12112(d)(3).
5. 29 C.F.R. § 1630.14(b)(3).
6. 42 U.S.C. § 12112(d)(4)(A).
7. *See* Knapp v. Northwestern Univ., 101 F.3d 473 (7th Cir. 1996).
8. Knapp v. Northwestern Univ., 101 F.3d 473 (7th Cir. 1996).
9. *See generally* discussion of direct threat in Chapter 1 of this book; *see also Chevron,* 536 U.S. 73 (2002).
10. *Chevron,* 536 U.S. at 86.
11. PGA Tour Inc. v. Martin, 532 U.S. 661 (2001).
12. *Id.* at 669.
13. *Id.* at 665-66.
14. *Id.* at 669.
15. *Id.*
16. *Id.* at 668.
17. *Id.*
18. *Id.*
19. *Id.*
20. *Id.* at 669.
21. *Id.*
22. *Id.* at 674.
23. *Id.*
24. *Id.* at 682.
25. *Id.* at 668.
26. *Id.* at 677, 680.
27. *Id.* at 676.
28. *Id.* at 677 n.24.
29. *Id.* at 677.
30. *Id.*
31. *Id.*
32. *Id.* at 678.
33. *Id.* at 679.
34. *Id.* at 680.
35. *Id.*
36. *Id.* at 683.
37. *Id.* at 684-85.
38. *Id.* at 685.
39. *Id.*
40. *Id.* at 686.
41. *Id.* at 685.
42. *Id.* at 685-86.
43. *Id.*
44. *Id.* at 686-87.
45. *Id.* at 687.
46. *Id.* at 690.
47. *Id.* at 689.

48. *Id*. at 690-91.
49. Hollenbeck v. Bd. of Educ. of Rochelle Twp., 699 F. Supp. 658 (N.D. Ill. 1988).
50. *Id*. at 661.
51. *Id.*
52. *Id*. at 668.
53. *Id*. at 666-67.
54. *Id*. at 668.
55. *See* Matthews v. NCAA, 179 F. Supp. 2d 1209, 1218-23 (E.D. Wash. 2001).
56. *See* 42 U.S.C. § 12182(b)(ii).
57. 42 U.S.C. § 12181(7)(L).
58. *PGA Tour*, 532 U.S. at 679-80.
59. Weyer v. Twentieth Century Fox Film Corp., 198 F.3d 1104 (9th Cir. 2000).
60. *See* Cook v. State of Rhode Island, 10 F.3d 17 (1st Cir. 1993).
61. *Id*. at 28.

Hot Areas 13

ADA AND MENTAL ILLNESS

Mᴇɴᴛᴀʟ ɪʟʟɴᴇss ɪs ʟɪᴋᴇʟʏ ᴛᴏ ʙᴇ ᴀ ʜᴏᴛ ᴀʀᴇᴀ for ADA litigation in the years to come for two reasons: First, mental illness often is not understood by employers. Second, the concepts of undue hardship and undue burden are very much focused on physical disabilities, as they often require some kind of equipment or auxiliary services. But what about the person with a mental illness? Most of the accommodations in the mental illness area cost very little, although at some point a fundamental alteration in the business may come into play. For example, a reasonable accommodation for a person with an anxiety disorder is to allow that person to take a five-minute break to regain his or her composure when the anxiety becomes overwhelming. The cost to the company is nominal. Another accommodation may be a job coach who is paid, directly or indirectly, through a state vocational rehabilitation agency. In short, many accommodations for mental illness involve staff time but no additional outlay of funds. Also, when dealing with the concept of mental illness, it must be remembered that the ADA does not permit discrimination where the work force is simply disrupted; the workplace must be fundamentally altered or result in an undue hardship, a far higher standard. Finally, in some cases, a duty may be created to step in and accommodate the illness.[1]

MENTAL RETARDATION

With respect to mental retardation, there are several areas of exposure that occur across Titles I, II, and III of the ADA. Many employers like to think their jobs require a certain degree of mental acuity. However, in truth, many jobs don't require much intellectual ability. If an employer were to use a prospective employee's low intelligence as the reason for not hiring that individual, the employer could run the risk of an ADA liability where it can be shown that intellectual acuity is simply not required for the particular job. This situation is no different from the problem, mentioned earlier in this book, that an employer faces when requiring a typing speed of seventy words a minute but in reality the job requires only fifty words a minute.

The issue of a governmental entity violating Title II of the ADA with regard to persons with mental retardation takes on various forms. For instance, a group home is audited in such a way that the disabilities of the residents are not taken into account. This can have disastrous consequences for the members of the home and for the provider, as it could lead to wrongfully decertifying the facility—a violation of Title II of the ADA.

Another area of exposure is prescribing medication to mentally retarded persons as a means of behavior control. This is commonplace and is a controversial medical practice. If there is no other reason for prescribing the medication than the person's disability, the practice could well violate the ADA, either Title II or III, depending on the circumstances.

The final area is the state practice of "warehousing" persons with mental illness and mental retardation in state institutions. The ADA uses very strong language in Title II and in its implementing regulations to suggest that failing to place a person with a disability in the most integrated setting appropriate to his or her needs is an ADA violation. In fact, at least one court, following up on the U.S. Supreme Court in *Olmstead v. L.C. by Zimring,* has held precisely that.[2]

Olmstead involved a suit by persons with disabilities claiming that it was a violation of Title II of the ADA to unnecessarily warehouse them in institutions.[3] The Supreme Court decided to hear the *Olmstead* case even though no other circuit had even reached the issue of the ADA's stance on the placement of persons with mental retardation and/or mental illness. It's hard to say why the Supreme Court decided to hear the case, because the justices had a difficult time reaching consensus. The case generated four different opinions: one opinion for the Court in which not all of the justices joined all the parts, a concurrence by Justice Stevens, a concurrence by Justice Kennedy, and a dissent by Justice Thomas.

The opinion for the Court, written by Justice Ginsburg, tried to stake out a middle ground between the two possible extremes: that the ADA did not apply to this situation at all or that the ADA mandated community integration of persons with mental illness and/or mental retardation. Instead, the Court decided that the ADA does require community integration when:

1. The state's treatment professionals have determined that community placement is appropriate.
2. The transfer to the less restrictive setting is not opposed by the affected individual.
3. The placement can be reasonably accommodated, taking into account the resources available to the state and the needs of others with mental disabilities.[4]

Elements one and two are very straightforward, but it is much harder to understand what Justice Ginsburg meant by element number three. Other aspects of the opinion for the Court are confusing as well. For example, as we have already discussed, a public entity does not have to accommodate a person with a disability if doing so would constitute an undue burden or a fundamental alteration to the nature of the program or activity of the public entity. I have always thought of undue burden and fundamental alteration as two different concepts. "Undue burden" signifies financial hardship, and "fundamental alteration" has to do with the way the program or activity operates. Yet Justice Ginsburg appears to use the term *fundamental alteration* as a synonym for *undue burden* when she specifically rules out looking at the entire mental health budget as the yardstick for measuring whether a particular reasonable accommodation is appropriate.[5] Justice Ginsburg says that a state utilizing the fundamental alteration defense should be allowed to show that in the allocation of available resources, immediate relief for the plaintiffs would not be fair, given the responsibility of the state for the care and treatment of a large and diverse population of persons with mental disabilities.[6]

Justice Ginsburg's discussion of what the state needs to show with a fundamental alteration defense is broad enough to wonder whether the state would not always prevail using such a defense, given how a state government often locks itself into set bureaucracies that are difficult to change. However, Justice Ginsburg appears to qualify these remarks at the conclusion of the opinion, which was not joined by all the justices, when she addresses how the state can satisfy its obligation to make reasonable accommodations to a person with a disability. Justice Ginsburg said that one way a state could demonstrate that it has made the appropriate reasonable modifications is to show that it has a comprehensive, effective plan for placing qualified persons with mental disabilities in less restrictive settings and a waiting list that moved at a reasonable pace not controlled by the state's desire to keep institutions fully populated.[7] Thus, from the majority opinion, we know that unnecessary segregation of persons with mental disabilities in institutions is prohibited by the ADA, but it is very unclear at what point the state has a sufficient defense to refuse to place a person with mental disabilities in a community program.[8]

Justice Stevens would have gone much further than Justice Ginsburg by simply voting to affirm the lower court decision.[9] Justice Stevens also mentions that there were not five votes for simply affirming the lower court's opinion.[10] Justice Stevens's mention of the difficulty of getting five votes for affirmance may go a long way toward explaining why certain aspects of Justice Ginsburg's opinion are hard to understand, as the opinion may have been written with consensus rather than bright lines in mind.

Justice Kennedy also filed a concurring opinion. Of particular note is his statement that a state without a community integration program in place is not required to create one.[11] Nevertheless, Justice Kennedy does say how he would go about deciding whether a state's community integration program passes muster under the Americans with Disabilities Act. He states that such a program would *not* pass under the ADA if (1) the state provides treatment to individuals suffering from medical problems of comparable seriousness; (2) as a general matter, such treatment is provided in the most integrated setting appropriate for the treatment of those problems after taking into account medical and other practical considerations; *but* (3) without adequate justification, fails to do so for a group of mentally disabled persons.[12]

Even this paradigm for deciding when a state's community integration program passes muster is confusing at times. For example, what does Justice Kennedy mean by "practical considerations"? What does he mean by "as a general matter"? And what does "adequate justification" mean? Perhaps there will be other decisions to come before the Court that will address those questions.

Finally, Justice Thomas filed a dissenting opinion in which the Chief Justice and Justice Scalia joined.

SEX CHANGE

This medical procedure raises a host of interesting issues. First, is the person who undergoes a sex change disabled under the ADA? The ADA and its implementing regulations makes clear that a person undergoing a sex change does not have a disability unless it is based on a physical condition.[13] Thus, a plaintiff would have to show that the sex change is related to a physical condition, a showing that might be very difficult to prove in light of the literature. The other possibility is that an employer could perceive the person undergoing a sex change as having a disability even though the person does not. Such perception, depending upon the Circuit, could activate the ADA and the reasonable accommodation requirement.[14] Finally, when dealing with this issue, the Family and Medical Leave Act must be considered, as it is likely that a sex change would be a "serious health condition."[15]

What preventive steps can an employer take to head off very public litigation over a sex change? First and foremost, make sure the staff knows that the person undergoing the sex change is to be treated as if he or she had never embarked on this procedure. For example, referring the person for a psychological examination invites disaster, as it strongly suggests that a disability is perceived. The employer must also take a request for leave under the FMLA very seriously. In fact, it might be a good idea to suggest the leave even if the person planning on the sex change doesn't think to ask for it.

INTERNET AND TITLE III OF THE ADA

Whether Title III's applicability is limited to physical structures is the $64,000 question when it comes to the boom in e-commerce. After all, many e-commerce businesses do not even have a place where the customer can go; their "place" is the Internet. For example, as of this writing, the author is aware of a suit against an online university for failure to accommodate a person with a disability. To hold that physical structure is the key would mean giving businesses that operate solely on the Internet carte blanche to discriminate against persons with disabilities when selling their goods and services. Such a holding is hardly equitable, but is there law to support such an inequitable result? The answer is yes and no. The case law breaks down into three views. First, there is the view that the Internet is simply not a place of public accommodation as set forth in *Access Now, Inc. v. Southwest Airlines Co.*[16] In *Access Now*, the Southern District of Florida held that Southwest Airlines did not have to make its Internet site accessible to persons with disabilities because Title III of the ADA is restricted in its coverage to physical places.[17] An opposite view, the Internet is a place of public accommodation, was stated by Justice Posner of the Seventh Circuit in *Doe v. Mutual of Omaha Insurance Company.*[18] While admittedly the statement that follows may not have been critical to the disposition of that case, it is noteworthy because of how convinced Justice Posner seems to be of his view of the scope of Title III of the ADA's nondiscrimination provision. Justice Posner, relying on *Carparts Distribution Center, Inc. v. Automotive Wholesaler's Association of New England,*[19] said:

> The core meaning of this provision [Title III of the ADA's non-discrimination provision], plainly enough, is that the owner or operator of a store, hotel, restaurant, dentist's office, travel agency, theater, *Web Site*, or other facility (*whether in physical space or in electronic space*) [citation to Carparts omitted] that is open to the public cannot exclude disabled persons from entering the facility and, once in, from using the facility in the same way that the nondisabled do.[20] (emphasis added)

Finally, there is a middle ground mentioned by the Ninth Circuit in *Weyer v. Twentieth Century Fox Film Corp.*[21] That ground essentially relies on a two-step approach: (1) Determine if a place of public accommodation as defined by Title III of the ADA is somehow involved; and (2) if the answer to the first question is in the affirmative, then assess whether a nexus exists between the event complained of and the place of public accommodation.[22]

The question of how Title III of the ADA applies to the Internet is not going to go away, especially as e-commerce takes over all of our lives. The ultimate question will have to be decided by the U.S. Supreme Court, and I would not want to hazard a guess as to how it might so decide this question.

LOVE BOAT

Ever taken a cruise? While this author has yet to do so, a few facts about cruises are well-known.

Various companies own and operate cruise lines, such as Norwegian, Carnival, Royal Holland, etc. These ships, essentially floating resorts,[23] sail from U.S. ports containing mainly U.S. passengers, over seven million by one count,[24] and go to various ports of call,[25] often in foreign countries. Ever notice the country's flag flying on the ship? For whatever reason, even though these ships are basically U.S.-centered ventures, it is most assuredly not the United States flag.[26] Should a ship carrying mainly U.S. passengers from U.S. ports of call and ending in U.S. ports of call be subject to the ADA when the flag it flies is not that of the United States? That was exactly the issue before the United States Supreme Court in *Spector v. Norwegian Cruise Line*.[27] In *Spector*, Spector and others claimed that the Norwegian Cruise Line required disabled passengers to pay higher fares and special surcharges that non-disabled passengers did not have to pay; maintained evacuation programs and equipment in locations not accessible to disabled individuals; required disabled individuals but not the non-disabled to waive any potential medical liability; required that disabled individuals travel with a companion; and reserved the right to remove from the ship any disabled individual whose presence endangered the comfort of other passengers.[28] Spector and others also pled in a more general way that the Norwegian Cruise Line failed to make reasonable modifications to policies, practices, and procedures necessary to ensure their full enjoyment of all the services offered.[29]

In a plurality opinion, a majority of the Court found that the ADA did apply to such vessels even though they carried a foreign flag of convenience, as long as the internal affairs (the Court also used the term "internal order and discipline") of the ship were not compromised.[30] However, the Court could not agree on what "internal affairs" meant.[31] In fact, Justice Kennedy in his opinion, for which he found a majority for portions of it, admitted that "internal affairs" is a category not always well defined and may require future judicial elaboration.[32]

The justices had varying views on what "internal affairs" might mean. Justice Kennedy, for example, believed that when it came to physical barriers for persons with disabilities on the ship, such a problem could well go to the internal affairs of the ship, as different countries might have different architectural requirements.[33] Justice Thomas clearly believed that the ADA would not be applicable to structural modifications, as that would go to the ship's internal affairs.[34] Justices Ginsburg and Souter believed that internal affairs only came into play where ADA would conflict with international obligations.[35] Both Ginsburg and Souter disagreed with the proposition that the internal affairs of a ship could include barrier modification if such barrier modification did not conflict with international law.[36]

So where does *Spector* leave us with respect to the ADA? It's confusing to try and piece together how the opinion breaks down among the justices. We can say this: If structural modifications are not involved, the disabled plaintiff has a much better shot at winning any ADA suit against a cruise line. Of course, with Chief Justice Roberts and Justice Samuel Alito being new to the Court, this all bears close watching and anything can happen.

NOTES

1. Sears Roebuck & Co., *supra*, 417 F.3d 789, 804.
2. *See* Penn. Prot. and Advocacy, Inc. v. Penn. Dep't of Public Welfare, 402 F.3d 374 (3d Cir. 2005).
3. L.C. By Zimring v. Olmstead, 138 F.3d 893, 895 (11th Cir. 1998); *see also* discussion of U.S. Supreme Court decision in this case, *supra* and *infra*.
4. Olmstead v. L.C. By Zimring, 527 U.S. 581, 607 (1999).
5. *Id.* at 603-04.
6. *Id.* at 604.

7. *Id.* at 605-06.
8. The courts are struggling as to when a state has a sufficient financial defense under *Olmstead* vis-á-vis what are now final federal rules requiring the integration of persons with disabilities into the community. For example, one court adopted several different parts of *Olmstead* to decide that the State of Pennsylvania had not presented as a matter of law a sufficient fundamental alteration defense. *See* Penn. Prot. and Advocacy, Inc. v. Penn. Dep't of Public Welfare, 402 F.3d 374 (3d Cir. 2005). Cases such as this one bear very close watching to see just how far a state's Title II obligations will extend with respect to the integration of persons with disabilities into the community.
9. *Olmstead, supra,* 527 U.S. at 607-08 (Stevens, J., concurring).
10. *Id.* at 608.
11. *Id.* at 612 (Kennedy, J., concurring).
12. *Id.*
13. 29 C.F.R. § 1630.3(d)(1).
14. *See* Kelly v. Metallics West, *supra,* 410 F.3d at 675, and the cases cited therein.
15. 29 C.F.R. § 825.114(a)(2).
16. Access Now, Inc. v. Southwest Airlines Co., 227 F. Supp. 2d 1312 (S.D. Fla. 2002).
17. *Id.* at 1319-21.
18. Doe v. Mutual of Omaha Ins. Co., 179 F.3d 557 (7th Cir. 1999).
19. Carparts Distrib. Center, Inc. v. Automotive Wholesaler's Ass'n of New England, 37 F.3d 12, 19 (1st Cir. 1994).
20. *Doe,* 179 F.3d at 559.
21. Weyer v. Twentieth Century Fox Film Corp., 198 F.3d 1104 (9th Cir. 2000).
22. *Id.* at 114-15.
23. Spector v. Norwegian Cruise Line, Ltd., _ U.S. _, 125 S. Ct. 2169, 162 L. Ed. 2d 97, 105 (2005).
24. *Id.* at 109.
25. *Id.* at 105.
26. *Id.* at 106.
27. *Spector, supra.*
28. *Id.* at 110.
29. *Id.*
30. *Id.*
31. The plurality in this case is quite complicated. One has to closely study what part of the opinion, which is divided into parts, a majority of justices agreed with. When one does that, it becomes apparent that there was only agreement as to the "internal affairs" language but not as to what it meant.
32. *Id.* at 110. (This particular statement comes from a section of the opinion for which there was no majority, though a reading of the of all the opin-

ions in the case would suggest that a majority of the justices would not disagree with the statement.

33.   *Id.* at 111.
34.   *Id.* at 120 (Thomas, J., concurring and dissenting).
35.   *Id.* at 116 (Ginsburg and Souter, JJ., concurring in part and concurring in the judgment).
36.   *Id.* at 117.

Are You Ready to Rock and Roll with Your ADA Case?

14

WHAT FOLLOWS ARE THREE CHECKLISTS for practitioners to use as they develop their ADA cases and prepare for trial. These checklists will help format discovery requests and serve as a reference point as the ADA case develops. They are divided into three categories: employment, operations of governmental entities, and places of public accommodation. The lists are not meant to be exhaustive, nor are they necessarily in any order of priority, but they serve as a starting point. Also included in this chapter are sample ADA forms. Those forms are offered by way of example and illustration and are not meant to substitute for the judgment of the litigator/individual attorney.

CHECKLIST 1: EMPLOYMENT

❑ Have you established that the plaintiff has a physical impairment?

❑ Have you established that the plaintiff has a mental impairment?

❑ Have you established that the plaintiff has a major life activity that is substantially limited?

❑ Is the major life activity of central importance to most people's daily lives?

> ❑ If a plaintiff is alleging that working is the affected major life activity. If representing plaintiff, are you absolutely sure there is no other major life activity that could have been relied upon?

❑ Have you investigated whether your Circuit has held whether substantial limitation of a major life activity means that regardless of the major life activity alleged, save working (see above), the plaintiff has to be severely restricted or prevented from performing a major life activity? Or has your Circuit limited the holding of *Toyota Motor* to the major life activity of performing manual tasks?

❑ Have you examined all applicable records to see if the plaintiff has a record of a disability?

❑ Have you analyzed the case to see if the plaintiff is perceived as having a physical or mental impairment and that the employer also perceives the plaintiff as being limited in a major life activity?

> ❑ If a perceived disability case is involved, have you investigated to see whether your jurisdiction demands that perceived disabilities be accommodated?

❑ If on the defense side, can you structure the case so that working becomes the major life activity that plaintiff relies upon?

❑ If on the defense side, can you convince the court that *Toyota Motor's* definition of what is a substantial limitation on a major life activity should be read to include all major life activities—again save working, which is governed by separate parameters?

❑ Does the plaintiff use mitigating measures? If so, have you checked whether your Circuit applies *Toyota Motor* to all major life activities, as discussed above, or does your Circuit limit it to performing manual tasks? If your Circuit does limit *Toyota Motor* to performing manual tasks, assuming the tasks alleged are not manual tasks, have you assessed how such mitigating measures are used and whether their use limits the plaintiff in performing that major life activity when compared to the average person without a disability? If *Toyota Motor* has not been so limited, have you considered whether, even with mitigating measures, plaintiff is severely restricted or prevented from performing that major life activity?

❏ Have you reached your conclusion based on objective or other factual evidence?

❏ Have you determined whether the plaintiff's disability is "temporary"?

❏ Have you determined that the plaintiff has the requisite skills, experience, and education for the position he/she holds or desires?

❏ Have you established that the plaintiff can perform the essential functions of the job he/she holds or desires with or without reasonable accommodations?

❏ Have you assessed whether the plaintiff is a direct threat to himself or others?

❏ Have you come to that conclusion based upon objective medical or other factual evidence?

❏ Have you determined whether the risk can be reduced to less than that of a direct threat by reasonable accommodations?

❏ Have you determined if the safety of others is one of the essential functions of the job?

❏ Have you received a right-to-sue letter from the EEOC?

❏ Have you determined what the essential functions of the job(s) are?

❏ Have you made sure in assessing the essential functions of the job(s) that they have not been confused with job tasks or with major life activities?

❏ In the course of analyzing the job's essential functions, have you determined what actually transpires?

❏ If the plaintiff affirmatively disclosed a disability in a pre-hire interview, have you determined the nature of the follow-up questions, if any, that were asked?

❏ If on the defense side, can you show instances of negotiating in good faith with the plaintiff to find a suitable reasonable accommodation? Can the client demonstrate a record of creativity in the quest to find a reasonable accommodation for the plaintiff?

❏ Have you assessed whether providing the reasonable accommodation would fundamentally alter the nature of the business?

❏ Have you assessed whether the employer can afford the accommodation? (Invariably a non-issue, but remains a theoretical possibility and even more so in light of *Olmstead*.)

❏ If on the defense side, are you sure the client understands that undue hardship does not equal inconvenience?

❏ If on the defense side, have you established that in the reasonable accommodation process the lines of communication were always kept open?

❏ Have you established that the plaintiff affirmatively disclosed to the employer that he/she had a disability?

❏ Have you investigated whether your Circuit is one that holds that the employer is put on notice of a disability if it is reasonable for it to know that the plaintiff was disclosing a disability even though the plaintiff may not have explicitly disclosed the disability?

❏ Have you determined whether the plaintiff is using illegal drugs or alcohol?

❏ Have you determined whether the plaintiff has ever been in an alcohol or drug rehabilitation program?

❏ Have you determined whether the plaintiff has a record of using drugs that went beyond casual use?

❏ Have you determined whether the plaintiff was asked any preemployment disability-related questions?

❏ Have you determined whether the defendant insisted on a full release to return to work?

❏ Have you analyzed the terms of the collective bargaining agreement or the company's seniority system to see how it addresses accommodating a person with a disability?

❏ If representing a union, are you satisfied that the union's interest and the union member's interests are aligned? If not, have appropriate steps been taken to satisfy fair representation obligations?

❏ Have you determined whether an impermissible medical exam occurred?

    ❏ Regardless of whether the person underwent a preemployment medical exam, have you analyzed whether that exam contained any preemployment medical or disability-related inquiries?

    ❏ If a post-employment medical exam is involved, have you determined whether the medical exam was job-related and consistent with business necessity?

❏ Have you determined if there was a conditional job offer? If so, and the offer was withdrawn, can it be shown that: (1) the reason for the withdrawal was job-related; (2) the reason for the withdrawal was consistent with business necessity; and (3) the medical exam revealed that the plaintiff cannot perform the essential functions of the job with or without reasonable accommodations?

❏ Have you reviewed the personnel file and the confidential medical information file? Have you determined whether medical information about the person's disability appears in the personnel file?

❏ If a Title I case, does the defendant have fifteen or more employees?

❏ If it appears the company has less than fifteen employees, have you applied the control test to see if employees not considered employees by the company are in fact employees under the case law?

❏ If on the defense side, have you determined whether the plaintiff applied for Social Security benefits, long-term disability benefits or short-term disability benefits? If so, have you reviewed the statements made in those applications to see if they jeopardize the plaintiff's request for an accommodation under the ADA?

    ❏ Have you established who told the plaintiff to apply for such benefits? Was it the employer?

❑ Do you have copies of the long-term and short-term disability benefits policies?

❑ Do you have copies of the representations made by the plaintiff during the course of seeking disability benefits?

❑ Have you read the U.S. Supreme Court opinion in *Cleveland v. Policy Management Systems Corp.*?

❑ If a plaintiff, have you considered bringing suit under ERISA? If a defendant, is the plaintiff's claim somehow preempted by ERISA?

❑ Have you analyzed the relationship between the ADA, the FMLA, and worker's compensation as it applies to your case?

❑ Have you considered that professional sports teams are employers under the ADA?

❑ Is your case a disparate impact case or a disparate treatment case, and are you aware of how each type of case is proven?

❑ Have you checked to see if the plaintiff has signed any arbitration agreement? If so, is the agreement written to include the ADA?

❑ If an employment matter is involved and the defendant is a state entity, has your state waived sovereign immunity?

❑ At trial, have you used *Batson* challenges to ensure that persons with disabilities are not excluded from the jury pool?

❑ If on the plaintiff's side, have you maximized your chances for obtaining attorney's fees per the case law?

CHECKLIST 2: OPERATIONS OF A GOVERNMENTAL ENTITY

❑ Have you established that the plaintiff has a physical impairment?

❑ Have you established that the plaintiff has a mental impairment?

❑ Have you established that the plaintiff has a major life activity that is substantially limited?

❑ Have you examined all applicable records to see if the plaintiff has a record of a disability?

❑ Have you analyzed the case to see if the plaintiff is perceived as having a physical or mental impairment?

❏ Have you analyzed the records to see if the plaintiff is perceived as substantially limited in one or more of life's major activities?

❏ If on the defense side, can you show that while the client perceived that the plaintiff suffered from an impairment, the client did not perceive that the plaintiff was substantially limited in any major life activity?

❏ Have you determined if a governmental entity is involved?

❏ If on the plaintiff's side, have you obtained a copy of the ADA internal grievance procedure, the self-evaluation plan, and the transition plan?

❏ Have you determined just what governmental program was denied to the plaintiff?

❏ If plaintiff, have you defined "program" as broadly as possible?

❏ If defendant, have you defined "program" as narrowly as reasonable?

❏ Have you determined whether the plaintiff can, with or without reasonable modifications to rules, policies, or practices; the removal of architectural, communication, or transportation barriers; or the provision of auxiliary services and aids, meet the essential eligibility requirements for the receipt of services or the participation in programs or activities provided by the governmental entity?

❏ Have you determined the essential eligibility requirements of the program at issue? Do these requirements screen out persons with disabilities?

❏ If on the defendant's side, can you establish that the accommodations asked for would fundamentally alter the nature of the program? (See *Easley v. Snider.*)

❏ If on the plaintiff's side, if a public entity claims undue burden, do you have a copy of the public entity's certification?

❏ If on the plaintiff's side, have you determined whether services are being provided in as integrated a setting as possible? (See *Olmstead v. L.C.*)

❏ Is an activity involved rather than a program? If on the defense side, where the activity is not accessible, can you show that the activity is just part of a larger program that is accessible?

❏ Have you determined the essential eligibility requirements of the activity?

❏ If on the plaintiff's side, have you amassed evidence to show that an adverse zoning decision was the result of stereotypical attitudes toward persons with disabilities or involved other forms of disability discrimination?

❏ Have you considered the applicability of the state and federal fair housing acts to your case?

❏ If on the plaintiff's side, have you exhausted all of the IDEA processes? If so, have you considered adding ADA causes of action to your case when you file in court?

❏ Have you made sure that punitive damages have not been alleged?

❏ If suing a state entity for discrimination outside of the employment context, have you researched the question of whether the discrimination at issue involved fundamental rights, basic rights, basic constitutional guarantees, or the administration of justice (assuming the state has not waived sovereign immunity).

❏ At trial, have you used *Batson* challenges to ensure that persons with disabilities are not excluded from the jury pool?

❏ If on the plaintiff's side, have you maximized your chances for obtaining attorney's fees per the case law?

CHECKLIST 3: PLACES OF PUBLIC ACCOMMODATION

❏ If the building was built after January 26, 1992, have you determined whether the facility satisfies ADA architectural standards?

❏ Have you assessed whether the facility, new or otherwise, meets state disability accessibility standards, where applicable?

❏ Have you determined whether any alterations were performed on the facility after January 26, 1992? If so, were the path of travel regulations complied with?

❏ Have you determined the nature of the business? Does it fit into one of the categories the ADA refers to as places of public accommodation? If not, is the business leasing out a place of public accommodation for its event? Also, if the answer is no, can you show a nexus between an entity in one of the categories and the discriminatory action complained of?

❏ Has the business begun to make readily achievable modifications to a facility built before January 26, 1992, as set forth in the Department of Justice regulations?

❏ Are auxiliary aids or services involved?

   ❏ If on the defense side, are you prepared to show an undue burden?

   ❏ If on the defense side, are you prepared to show that the requested accommodation would fundamentally alter the nature of the business operation?

❏ Have you assessed whether the business is controlled by a religious entity?

❏ If the business itself is not a place of public accommodation, have you assessed whether a portion of the business is a place of public accommodation?

❏ Have you considered the applicability of federal and state fair housing acts?

❏ If a building was built after January 26, 1992, and does not meet ADA accessibility regulations, have you considered suing the architect on two grounds: (1) directly for malpractice (plaintiff or defense side) and (2) under Title III of the ADA (plaintiff's side)?

❏ Have you obtained a copy of the lease between the business and the landlord?

❏ Have you considered bringing suit under Title III of the ADA even when the plaintiff was not physically on the premises when denied access to the business? If so, have you considered whether the business is strictly online or does it have a physical place of business that people can access?

❏ Have you drafted your lease to account for complying with the ADA?

❏ If on the plaintiff's side, have you maximized your chances for obtaining attorney's fees per the case law?

Appendix: Pleadings (Sample Complaints and Answers)

LITIGATION FORMS (The Defense View)

Answer (Title I)

Defendants _____, by and through their attorneys, _____, as their Answer to Plaintiff's complaint in the above-captioned cause, hereby deny each and every allegation contained therein except as expressly delineated below.

Notice of Action
This is an action under Title I of the Americans with Disabilities Act of 1990 ("ADA") to redress unlawful disability-based employment practices and to make plaintiff, (name of plaintiff), whole. Defendant, (name of defendant), discharged plaintiff, a qualified individual with a disability, (state disability), from his position as (state title of position), because of his disability.
Answer: Defendant admits that this is an action filed under Title I of the Americans with Disabilities Act of 1990 (hereafter ADA). Defendant denies committing unlawful employment practices or taking adverse action against

plaintiff because of a disability, as defined by the ADA, or that any alleged disability of plaintiff was a motivating factor in the adverse employment decision. Defendant also denies that plaintiff was a qualified individual with a disability at the time the adverse action was taken. Defendant further denies that plaintiff was a person with a disability as defined by the ADA.

Jurisdiction and Venue

1. Jurisdiction of this court is proper under 28 U.S.C. 451, 1331, 1337, and 1343. This action is instituted under Section 107(a) of the ADA, 42 U.S.C. 12,117—incorporating by reference Sections 706(f)(1),(3) of Title VII of the Civil Rights Act of 1964 ("Title VII"), 42 U.S.C. 2000e–5(f)(1),(3).

   Answer: Defendant admits the allegations contained in paragraph 1 of plaintiff's Jurisdiction and Venue section of this complaint.

2. The alleged unlawful employment practices took place and are taking place in the _____ District of _____, _____ Division.

   Answer: Defendant denies that any unlawful employment practices have taken place or are taking place. Defendant admits that it does conduct business in the _____ District of _____, _____ Division.

Parties

3. (name of plaintiff) is an otherwise qualified individual with a disability who was employed by (name of defendant) from _____ to _____.

   Answer: Defendant denies that plaintiff is an otherwise qualified individual with a disability. Defendant further denies that plaintiff has a disability as defined in the ADA. [Alternatively, defendant lacks sufficient information or knowledge as to whether plaintiff has a disability as defined by the ADA and therefore: a) demands that plaintiff be put to his/her proof, and b) denies same.]

4. Plaintiff is expressly authorized under Section 107(a) of the ADA, 42 U.S.C. 12,117—incorporating by reference Sections 706(f)(1),(3) of Title VII of the Civil Rights Act of 1964 ("Title VII"), 42 U.S.C. 2000e–5(f)(1),(3)—to bring this action.

Answer: Defendant admits.

5. At all relevant times, (name of defendant) has been a corporation doing business in (state and city), and at all relevant times (name of defendant) has had at least 15 employees.
Answer: Defendant admits.

6. At all relevant times, (name of defendant) has been engaged in an industry affecting commerce within the meaning of Section 101(5) of the ADA, 42 U.S.C. 12,111(5).
Answer: Defendant admits. {Defendant denies that it is engaged in an industry affecting commerce.}*
* Hard to believe that this could be a possible defense, especially with the Internet thrown into the equation, but it is mentioned here as at least a theoretical possibility.

7. At all relevant times, (name of defendant) has been a covered entity under Section 101(2) of the ADA, 42 U.S.C. 12,111(2).
Answer: Defendant admits. [Defendant denies.]

Statement of Claims

8. (Name of plaintiff) has exhausted his/her administrative remedies by timely filing a charge with the Equal Employment Opportunity Commission alleging violations of Title I of the ADA by (name of defendant) and obtaining a right to sue letter from the EEOC. All conditions precedent to the institution of this lawsuit have been fulfilled.
Answer: Defendant admits. {If right-to-sue letter has not been issued, then deny. Also may wish to deny if plaintiff is under a collective bargaining agreement and the terms of that agreement have not been exhausted.}

9. Since at least (date), (name of defendant) has engaged in unlawful employment practices in violation of ADA sections (list specific sections of Title I of the ADA that were violated) at (place where the ADA violations occurred). These practices include but are not limited to discharge of (name of plaintiff), an individual with a disability able to do the essential functions of the job with or without reasonable accommodations.
Answer: Defendant denies that it has engaged in unlawful employment practices in violation of the ADA. Defendant denies that it committed any of the alleged practices complained

of in paragraph number 9 of plaintiff's complaint. Defendant denies that plaintiff was able to perform the essential functions of his position with or without reasonable accommodation.

10. The effect of the practices complained of above has been to deprive (<u>name of plaintiff</u>) of equal employment opportunities and otherwise adversely affect his status as an employee because of his disability.

    Answer: *Defendant denies that plaintiff has been deprived of equal employment opportunities or otherwise adversely affected as an employee because of his alleged disability. Defendant further alleges that plaintiff's alleged disability was not a motivating factor in any alleged adverse employment decision against the plaintiff.*

11. The unlawful employment practices complained of herein were and are intentional.

    Answer: *Defendant denies that any unlawful employment practices complained of occurred. Defendant further avers that if any such practices did occur, such practices were not intentional.*

Defenses

13. Plaintiff has failed to state a claim upon which relief may be granted.

14. Defendant asserts that plaintiff was terminated for reasons related to job performance and not to disability. Plaintiff's disability was not a factor considered in terminating plaintiff's employment.

15. Defendant asserts that plaintiff was not a person with a disability as defined by the ADA.

16. Defendant asserts that plaintiff was not an otherwise qualified individual with a disability at the time of termination.

17. Even if plaintiff has a disability as defined by the ADA, defendant asserts that it in good faith attempted to reasonably accommodate plaintiff's disability and that plaintiff did not accept the proffered accommodations. Alternatively or in combination, defendant also alleges that plaintiff failed to engage in reasonable accommodation efforts in good faith.

18. Defendant asserts that to accommodate plaintiff would have fundamentally altered the nature of its business operations.
19. Defendant asserts that plaintiff presented a direct threat to the health and safety of him-/herself or to others at the time the plaintiff was terminated, denied promotion, demoted, etc. (Also refer to Chapter 1 of the text.)
20. Defendant asserts that plaintiff's admissions in his/her application for disability benefits has estopped plaintiff from proceeding with his/her claim under the ADA. [**Note:** Be sure to read the Supreme Court opinion in *Cleveland v. Policy Management Systems Corp.*]
21. Defendant asserts that to accommodate plaintiff would constitute an undue hardship.
22. Defendant alleges that it is in receipt of evidence obtained after plaintiff was terminated. That evidence, if known to defendant at time of termination, would have resulted in plaintiff's termination in any event. Therefore, any damages suffered by plaintiff as a result of the alleged discrimination should be limited accordingly.

Prayer for Relief

WHEREFORE, defendant, by and through its attorney, _____, prays that this Court dismiss the complaint filed in this cause and the Court grant the defendant such relief, equitable or at law, as the Court should so decide.

Answer (Title II)

Defendant _____, *by and through its attorneys,* _____, *as its answer to plaintiff's complaint in the above-captioned cause, hereby denies each and every allegation contained therein except as expressly delineated below.*

Nature of Action
This is an action under Title II of the Americans with Disabilities Act of 1990 ("ADA") and under Section 505 of the Rehabilitation Act of 1973, which enforces Section 504 of the Rehabilitation Act of 1973

("Rehabilitation Act"), to redress unlawful disability-based practices and to make plaintiff, (name of plaintiff), whole. Defendant, (name of defendant), denied (name of plaintiff) access to (name of defendant and name of defendant's program, activity or service) because of his disability.

Answer: Defendant admits that this is an action under Section 505 of the Rehabilitation Act of 1973 and Title II of the Americans with Disabilities Act of 1990 (ADA). Defendant denies that plaintiff was denied access to its programs and activities because of unlawful disability discrimination or that plaintiff suffered unlawful disability discrimination.

Jurisdiction and Venue

1. Jurisdiction of this court is proper under 28 U.S.C. 451, 1331, 1337, and 1343. This action is brought under Sections 202 and 203 of the ADA, 42 U.S.C. 12,132 and 12,133—incorporating by reference the remedies, procedures and rights under the Rehabilitation Act, 29 U.S.C. 794 and 794a—and under Section 505 of the Rehabilitation Act, which enforces Section 504 of the Rehabilitation Act, 42 U.S.C. 794 and 794a—incorporating the remedies, rights and procedures set forth in Section 717 of the Civil Rights Act of 1964, including the application of Sections 706(f) through 706(k), 42 U.S.C. 2000e–5(f)–(k).

   Answer: Defendant admits that this action is brought under Title II of the ADA and Section 505 of the Rehabilitation Act of 1973.

2. The alleged unlawful practices were and are taking place in the _____ District of _____, _____ Division.

Answer: Defendant denies that the practices alleged in plaintiff's complaint are unlawful. Defendant admits that they do conduct business in the _____ District of _____, _____ Division.

Parties

3. (Name of plaintiff) is an otherwise qualified individual with a disability, (state disability), who was denied access to (name of defendant) (name of defendant's program or activity) on or about (date).

> *Answer: Defendant denies that plaintiff is an otherwise quali-
> fied individual with a disability. Defendant further avers that it
> does not possess sufficient facts to state whether plaintiff is a
> person with a disability as defined by the ADA and therefore
> denies same. Therefore, defendant demands plaintiff be put to
> his proof. {Alternative: Defendant denies that plaintiff is a per-
> son with a disability as defined under the ADA.}*

4. Plaintiff is expressly authorized under Sections 202 and 203
   of the ADA, 42 U.S.C. 12,132 and 12,133—incorporating by
   reference the remedies, procedures, and rights under the Rehabilitation Act, 29 U.S.C. 794 and 794a, and under Section
   505 of the Rehabilitation Act, which enforces Section 504 of
   the Rehabilitation Act, 42 U.S.C. 794 and 794a—incorporating the remedies, rights, and procedures set forth in Section
   717 of the Civil Rights Act of 1964, including the application
   of Sections 706(f) through 706(k), 42 U.S.C. 2000e–5(f)–(k),
   to bring this action.

   Answer: Defendant admits.

5. At all relevant times, (name of defendant) has been a public
   entity as defined in Section 201 of the ADA, 42 U.S.C.
   12,131(1).

   Answer: Defendant admits.

6. At all relevant times (name of defendant) has received federal
   funds.

   *Answer: Defendant admits {denies if defendant doesn't receive
   federal funding}.*

7. Since at least (date), (name of defendant) has engaged in unlawful practices in violation of ADA Sections (list specific sections of Title II of the ADA that were violated) and in violation
   of Section 504 of the Rehabilitation Act, 42 U.S.C. 794. These
   practices include but are not limited to denying (name of plaintiff)—an individual with a disability who, with or without reasonable modifications to rules, policies, or practices; the
   removal of architectural, communication, or transportation
   barriers; or the provision of auxiliary aids and services, meets
   the essential eligibility requirements for the receipt of services
   or the participation in programs or activities provided by (name
   of defendant)—access to the (name of program, service or
   activity) of (name of defendant).

Answer: Defendant denies the allegations that it has engaged in unlawful practices in violation of Title II of the ADA or in violation of Section 504–505 of the Rehabilitation Act of 1973. Defendant denies that plaintiff can, with or without reasonable modifications to rules, policies, or practices; the removal of architectural, communication, or transportation barriers; or the provision of auxiliary aids and services, meet the essential eligibility requirements for the receipt of services or the participation in programs or activities that defendant is alleged to have denied plaintiff access to. Defendant further avers that admitting plaintiff to defendant's (<u>name of program or activity</u>) would result in a fundamental alteration in the nature of the program/activity.

8. The effect of the practices complained of has been to deprive (<u>name of plaintiff</u>) equal access to a public entity's services, programs, and activities and to otherwise adversely affect his/her status as a member of the public interested in accessing (<u>name of defendant</u>)'s programs and activities.

   Answer: Defendant denies that plaintiff has been denied equal access to defendant's programs and activities.

Defenses

1. Plaintiff has failed to state a claim upon which relief may be granted.

2. Defendant denies that plaintiff is a person with a disability as defined by the ADA.

3. Defendant denies that plaintiff can, with or without reasonable modifications to rules, policies, or practices; the removal of architectural, communication or transportation barriers; or the provision of auxiliary aids and services, meet the essential eligibility requirements for the receipt of services or the participation in defendant's (<u>name of programs or activities</u>).

4. Defendant alleges in the alternative that if plaintiff is a person with a disability, that to admit plaintiff to defendant's (<u>name of program or activity</u>) would fundamentally alter the nature of the program or activity.

5. Defendant avers that its executive director certified that the requested accommodation was an undue hardship [inserted

here as a theoretical defense, though it is unlikely to occur in practice].

6. Defendant avers that plaintiff was offered numerous accommodations and turned those accommodations down.

7. Defendant denies that it receives federal funding [inserted here as a theoretical defense, though it is unlikely to occur in practice].

8. Defendant denies that plaintiff has construed defendant's program correctly. Rather, plaintiff was denied access to _____ (state defendant's view of program). Alternatively, defendant avers that plaintiff was denied access to an activity that is part of a larger program, which is readily accessible to plaintiff.

Prayer for Relief

WHEREFORE, defendant, by and through its attorneys, _____, prays that this Court dismiss the complaint filed in this cause and the Court grant the defendant such relief, equitable or at law, as the Court should so decide.

TITLE III (ANSWER)

(Seeking injunctive relief for discrimination by a place of public accommodation)

Nature of Action

This is an action under Title III of the Americans with Disabilities Act of 1990 ("ADA") to enjoin unlawful disability-based discrimination. Plaintiff, (name of plaintiff), was discriminated against on the basis of disability so that he was denied the full and equal enjoyment of the goods, services, facilities, privileges, advantages, or accommodations of a place of public accommodation owned, leased, or operated by the defendants, (name of defendants).

Answer: Defendants admit that this is an action under Title III of the Americans with Disabilities Act of 1990 (ADA). Defendants deny that plaintiff has suffered discrimination on account of disability as defined by the ADA.

Jurisdiction and Venue

1. Jurisdiction of this court is proper under 28 U.S.C. 451, 1331, 1337, and 1343. This action is brought under Section 308 of the ADA, 42 U.S.C. 12,188(a)—incorporating by reference the remedies and procedures found in 42 U.S.C. 2000a–3, Section 204 of the Civil Rights Act of 1964.
Answer: Defendants admit.

2. The alleged unlawful practices were and are now being committed in the _____ District of _____, _____ Division.
Answer: Defendants deny that any unlawful practices were or are now being committed. Defendants admit that they conduct business in the _____ District of _____, _____ Division.

PARTIES

3. (Name of plaintiff) is a person with a disability, (state nature of disability), who was denied the full and equal enjoyment of the goods, services, facilities, privileges, advantages, or accommodations of a place of public accommodation owned, leased, or operated by the defendants.
Answer: Defendants lack sufficient information to determine whether plaintiff is a person with a disability as defined by the ADA and therefore leave plaintiff to his/her proof. Defendants further deny that plaintiff was denied the full and equal enjoyment of defendants' facilities.

4. Name of plaintiff is expressly authorized under Section 308 of the ADA, 42 U.S.C. 12,188(a)—incorporating by reference the remedies and procedures found in 42 U.S.C. 2000a–3, Section 204 of the Civil Rights Act of 1964, to bring this action.
Answer: Defendants admit.

5. At all relevant times (name of defendant A) has been the owner/lessor of (location of the place of public accommodation).
Answer: Defendant admits that it has been the owner/lessor of (name of business). Defendant denies that it operates a place of public accommodation as defined by Title III of the ADA.

6. At all relevant times (name of defendant B) has been the operator of (name of the place of public accommodation).

Answer: Defendant admits that it has operated (name of business) but denies that it is a place of public accommodation.

7. (Name of the place of public accommodation) at all relevant times has been a place of public accommodation in that it is a place of public accommodation under (select applicable type of public accommodation as set forth in 42 U.S.C. 12,181(7). Include its corresponding statutory reference.).

Answer: Defendants deny that it is a place of public accommodation. {It is of course possible that the facts of the case are such that it is clear a place of public accommodation is involved.}

Statement of Claims

8. Since at least (date), (names of all defendants) have engaged in unlawful practices in violation of ADA Sections (list specific sections of Title III of the ADA that were violated). These practices include but are not limited to (list the incidents of discrimination by each defendant).

Answer: Defendants deny that they have engaged in unlawful practices in violation of the ADA and that any of its practices violated the ADA.

9. The effect of the practices complained of has been to deprive (name of plaintiff) the full and equal enjoyment of a place of public accommodation and to otherwise adversely affect his/her status as a member of the public interested in accessing the place of public accommodation owned, leased, and/or operated by the defendants, (names of defendants).

Answer: Defendants deny that plaintiff has lost the full and equal enjoyment of a place of public accommodation and deny otherwise adversely affecting plaintiff's status as a member of the public interested in accessing the defendants' place of business/facility.

Defenses

1. Plaintiff has failed to state a claim under which relief can be granted.
2. Defendants deny that they operate a place of public accommodation as defined by Title III of the ADA.

3. Defendants deny that plaintiff has a disability as defined by the ADA.

4. Even if plaintiff has a disability under the ADA, defendants aver that the modifications requested by plaintiff would not be readily achievable.

5. Even if plaintiff has a disability under the ADA, defendants aver that the auxiliary aids and services requested by plaintiff would, if provided, constitute an undue burden on defendants.

6. Even if plaintiff has a disability under the ADA, defendants aver that providing the auxiliary aids and services requested by the plaintiff would result in a fundamental alteration in the nature of defendants' business.

7. Defendants aver that the facility plaintiff complains of being denied access to is a facility on the National Register of Historic Places.

Prayer for Relief

WHEREFORE, defendants, by and through their attorneys, _____, pray that this Court dismiss the complaint filed in this cause and the Court grant the defendants such relief, equitable or at law, as the Court should so decide.

DEFENDANT'S REQUEST TO PRODUCE

Pursuant to Rule 34, Defendant requests that the following documents be produced at the offices of _____, located at _____ on _____, for the purpose of inspection and copying by the Defendant.

1. Any and all medical records involving Plaintiff's alleged disabilities, including but not limited to (list physical or mental impairment being complained of) (list physical/mental impairments which you are aware of that Plaintiff has or had).

2. Any and all medical records involving Plaintiff's use of mitigating measures used in relation to each and every one of Plaintiff's alleged disabilities.

3. Any and all records kept by the entity supplying the Plaintiff with his or her prosthetic device, medications, or other mitigating measures.

4. Any and all records regarding Plaintiff's educational background.

5. Copies of any applications, statements, or written materials made by the Plaintiff in the course of applying for short-term and/or long-term disability benefits or made in the course of applying for Supplemental Social Security Income (SSI), Supplemental Social Security Disability Income (SSDI),or state disability programs.

6. Any and all medical records of the Plaintiff. Include both hospital and physician records.

7. Any and all psychiatric records of Plaintiff.

8. Any and all prescription records of Plaintiff.

9. Any and all employment records of Plaintiff prior to and subsequent to the time Plaintiff was in defendant's employ.

10. Copies of the lease between (<u>owner of place of public accommodation or governmental entity and the lessor of same</u>).

11. All documents relating to any alleged request by Plaintiff to Defendant for reasonable accommodation.

12. All documents identify what Plaintiff contends are the essential functions of his/her job.

13. All documents submitted by Plaintiff to the Equal Employment Opportunity Commission regarding his/her Charge of Discrimination filed on or about [date].

14. All document relating to any effort on Plaintiff' part to find a job at any time since [date].

15. All documents relating to payments that Plaintiff has received from any source since [date].

16. All documents relating in any way to Plaintiff's claim for workers' compensation.

17. All documents itemizing, supporting, or referencing any of Plaintiff's claimed damages in this lawsuit.

Defendant's Interrogatories

The Defendant requests that the following interrogatories be answered under oath by Plaintiff.

Definitions:

Disability—A person has a disability if he/she has a physical or mental impairment that substantially limits one or more of life's major activities, has a record of such an impairment, or is perceived as having such an impairment.

Physical/Mental Condition—The plaintiff's physical or mental status.

1. Describe in detail all physical/mental impairments that you had while employed at Defendants. Include but do not limit the description to those physical/mental impairments that you claim as the basis for disability discrimination and those physical/mental impairments that you claim may have been aggravated by your employment with Defendants.

2. State the name of each practitioner who has treated your physical/mental impairments. As to each such practitioner, state: A) the name, address and specialty; B) the date of each examination or treatment; C) the physical/mental impairment for which each examination or treatment was performed.

3. Describe how the physical/mental impairments referenced in question 1 above substantially limit a major life activity.

4. Since leaving Defendants' employ, has Plaintiff been hospitalized for any physical/mental impairment? If so: A) state the name and location of each hospital where the plaintiff was hospitalized; B) the date of each hospitalization; C) the conditions treated during each hospitalization; D) the nature of the treatment rendered during each hospitalization.

5. Is the Plaintiff still under the care of a medical practitioner? If so, state: A) the name and address of each practitioner; B) the nature of each condition being treated by the practitioner; C) the medical specialty of each practitioner; D) which of the conditions are related to the physical/mental impairments that Plaintiff had while in the employ of Defendants, and whether any of those conditions are a part of Plaintiff's claim of having a disability.

6. State for each medical expense stemming from treatment of Plaintiff's mental or physical impairment: A) the amount; B) the name and address of the person or entity paid or owed for the service; C) the date of each expense.

7. State whether Plaintiff has filed for: A) Supplemental Social Security Income (SSI); B) long-term disability benefits; C) short-term disability benefits. Also, state whether said application(s) was granted.

8. If Plaintiff has applied for short- or long-term disability benefits, state the name of the company administering the short-term or long-term disability benefits program.

9. List each job or employment held by Plaintiff since termination from Defendant's employ. State the following: A) name and address of employer; B) dates worked at each employer; C) nature of employment and duties; D) name, address, and title of immediate supervisor; E) rate of pay or compensation; F) reason for leaving/termination.

10. List each job or employment held by Plaintiff for the five years before becoming employed by Defendant. State: A) name and address of employer or entity hiring the person for a job; B) date of employment or length of the job; C) place of employment or where the job took place; D) nature of employment and duties performed; E) name and address of immediate supervisor; F) rate of compensation; G) reason for leaving/termination.

11. Does the Plaintiff claim that, as a result of termination from Defendant's employ, he/she has lost opportunities for advancement or promotion in his/her line of work? If so, state what opportunities would have been available had the alleged discrimination not occurred.

12. Does the Plaintiff take any medication for his/her disability? If so, state: A) the name of each medication taken and its dosage; B) whether there are any side effects to Plaintiff from taking the medication, and describe same; C) how the medication so taken impacts on Plaintiff's daily living activities.

13. Describe Plaintiff's job search after termination from Defendant's employ, including all jobs applied for, addresses of entities to which resumes were sent, and all employment agencies contacted.

14. Does the Plaintiff wear any prosthetic devices, take any medication, or engage in any other mitigating measures related to his/her physical or mental impairments? If so, state: A) the nature of each prosthetic device, medication, mitigating mea-

sure, how the prosthetic device is built or constructed, and how it operates; B) any side effects Plaintiff suffers as the result of the use of such device, medication(s), or other mitigating measure; C) how the prosthetic device, medication(s), or other mitigating measure impacts on Plaintiff's daily living activities.

15. Describe Plaintiff's educational history.

16. Identify what Plaintiff/Defendant believes to be the essential elements of the position Plaintiff held while in Defendant's employ. Describe how your conclusion was reached.

17. Identify all reasonable accommodations that you contend would enable you to perform the essential functions of your job.

18. Explain how each of the reasonable accommodations that you identified in Interrogatory No. ___ would enable you to perform the essential functions of your job.

19. Identify all documents that support your belief that the reasonable accommodations that you identified in Interrogatory No. ___ would enable you to perform the essential functions of your job.

LITIGATION FORMS (The Plaintiff's View)

TITLE I (COMPLAINT)

Nature of Action

This is an action under Title I of the Americans with Disabilities Act of 1990 ("ADA") to redress unlawful disability-based employment practices and to make plaintiff, (name of plaintiff), whole. Defendant, (name of defendant), discharged plaintiff, a qualified individual with a disability, (state disability), from his position as (state title of position), because of his disability. [Also, if desired, include state law supplemental claims here and throughout.]

Jurisdiction and Venue

1. Jurisdiction of this court is proper under 28 U.S.C. 451, 1331, 1337, and 1343. This action is instituted under Section 12,117(a) of the ADA, 42 U.S.C. 12,117—incorporating by reference Sections 706(f)(1),(3) of Title VII of the Civil Rights

Act of 1964 ("Title VII"), 42 U.S.C. 2000e–5(f)(1),(3). (*If alleging violation of Civil Rights Act, cover that as well. Also, if the defendant receives federal funding, consider alleging violations of Section 504 of the Rehabilitation Act of 1973.*) Venue is proper in this district under 28 U.S.C. 1391.

2. The alleged unlawful employment practices took place and are taking place in the _____ District of _____, _____ Division.

Parties

3. Plaintiff (<u>name of plaintiff</u>) is an individual with a disability in that Plaintiff has a physical or mental impairment (<u>state impairment</u>) that substantially limits the major life activity of _____ (<u>state major life activity</u>)

4. Plaintiff is an otherwise qualified individual with a disability in that Plaintiff was able to perform all of the essential functions of the job of _____ (state position), with or without reasonable accommodations.

5. Plaintiff was employed by Defendant (<u>name of defendant</u>) from _____ to _____.

4. Plaintiff is expressly authorized under Section 12,117(a) of the ADA, 42 U.S.C. 12,117—incorporating by reference Sections 706(f)(1),(3) of Title VII of the Civil Rights Act of 1964 ("Title VII"), 42 U.S.C. 2000e–5(f)(1),(3)—to bring this action.

5. At all relevant times, (<u>name of defendant</u>) has been a corporation doing business in (<u>state and city</u>), and at all relevant times (<u>name of defendant</u>) has had at least 15 employees.

6. At all relevant times, (<u>name of defendant</u>) has been engaged in an industry affecting commerce within the meaning of Section 101 (5) of the ADA, 42 U.S.C. 12,111(5).

7. At all relevant times, (<u>name of defendant</u>) has been a covered entity under Section 12,111(2) of the ADA, 42 U.S.C. 12,111(2).

Statement of Claims

8. On _____ (date of EEOC filing), (<u>name of plaintiff</u>) filed a charge with the Equal Employment Opportunity Commission alleging violations of Title I of the ADA by (<u>name of defendant</u>). Plaintiff has exhausted all available administrative remedies prior to the filing of this complaint.

9. On the following occasions, plaintiff requested accommodations for his disability: (list each occasion and what accommodations were requested).

10. Since at least (date), (name of defendant) has engaged in unlawful employment practices in violation of ADA sections (list specific sections of Title I of the ADA that were violated) at (place where the ADA violations occurred). These practices include but are not limited to denial of accommodation, denial of promotions, denial of employment benefits, and/or discharge of (name of plaintiff), an individual with a disability able to do the essential functions of the job with or without reasonable accommodations. [Plead disability and perceived disability in the alternative. Also, if you plead perceived disability, you will have to show that the defendant perceived a substantial limitation in a major life activity and might want to plead that as well.]

11. The effect of the practices complained of above has been to deprive (name of plaintiff) of equal employment opportunities and otherwise adversely affect his status as an employee because of his disability.

12. The unlawful employment practices complained of herein were and are intentional.

Prayer for Relief

WHEREFORE, the plaintiff respectfully requests that this court:

A. Grant a permanent injunction enjoining (name of defendant), its owners, officers, management personnel, employees, agents, successors, assigns, and in participation with them, from engaging in any employment practices that discriminate on the basis of disability;

B. Order (name of defendant) to institute and carry out policies, practices, and programs that provide equal employment opportunities to qualified individuals with disabilities and eradicate the effects of past and present unlawful employment practices;

C. Order (name of defendant) to make (name of plaintiff) whole by providing him with appropriate lost earnings and insurance premiums, with pre-judgment interest, in amounts to be proved at trial, and other affirmative relief necessary to eradicate the effects of its unlawful employment practices, including but not limited to reinstatement of (name of plaintiff) to the position of (title of position held by plaintiff);

D. Order (name of defendant) to make (name of plaintiff) whole by providing compensation for pecuniary losses, including but not limited to costs to be incurred for health and life insurance premiums and costs of seeking new employment, in amounts to be determined at trial;

E. Order (name of defendant) to remit payment to (name of plaintiff) for future prospective loss of pay for a period of time following the filing of the complaint;

F. Grant such further relief as the Court deems appropriate;

G. Grant the plaintiff his/her fees and costs in this action.

Note: In an employment case under Title I of the ADA, the Civil Rights Act of 1991 prohibits punitive damages against a governmental entity. Where a governmental entity is not involved in an employment matter under Title I of the ADA, the attorney may want to consider asking for punitive damages where appropriate.

Jury Demand

Plaintiff demands trial by jury.

TITLE II (COMPLAINT)

(Denial of Access to Governmental Services, Programs, and Activities)

Nature of Action

This is an action under Title II of the Americans with Disabilities Act of 1990 ("ADA") and under Section 505 of the Rehabilitation Act of 1973, which enforces Section 504 of the Rehabilitation Act of 1973 ("Rehabilitation Act"), to redress unlawful disability-based practices and to make plaintiff, (name of plaintiff), whole. Defendant, (name of defendant), denied (name of plaintiff) access to (name of defendant's and name of defendant's program, activity or service denied access to) because of his disability.

[Depending on the nature of the case and the applicable case law, there may be times when an attorney will elect to proceed solely under the ADA even where the defendant takes federal funds.]
[If architectural accessibility is involved, you may also have violation of state building codes.]

Jurisdiction and Venue

1. Jurisdiction of this court is proper under 28 U.S.C. 451, 1331, 1337, and 1343. This action is brought under Sections 12,132 and 12,133 of the ADA, 42 U.S.C. 12,132 and 12,133—incorporating by reference the remedies, procedures, and rights under the Rehabilitation Act, 29 U.S.C. 794 and 794a, and under Section 505 of the Rehabilitation Act, which enforces Section 504 of the Rehabilitation Act, 42 U.S.C. 794 and 794a—incorporating the remedies, rights, and procedures set forth in Section 717 of the Civil Rights Act of 1964, including the application of Sections 706(f) through 706(k), 42 U.S.C. 2000e–5(f)–(k).

2. The alleged unlawful practices were and are taking place in the _____ District of _____, _____Division.

Parties

3. (Name of plaintiff) is an individual with a disability in that Plaintiff has a physical or mental impairment (state impairment) that substantially limits the major life activity of (state major life activity).

4. Plaintiff is an otherwise qualified individual with a disability in that Plaintiff is qualified to access defendant's program or activity.

5. Plaintiff was denied access to (name of defendant) (name of defendant's program or activity) on or about (date).

4. Plaintiff is expressly authorized under Sections 12,132 and 12,133 of the ADA, 42 U.S.C. 12,132 and 12,133—incorporating by reference the remedies, procedures and rights under the Rehabilitation Act, 29 U.S.C. 794 and 794a—and under Section 505 of the Rehabilitation Act, which enforces Section 504 of the Rehabilitation Act, 42 U.S.C. 794 and 794a—incorporating the remedies, rights and procedures set forth in Section 717 of the Civil Rights Act of 1964, including the ap-

plication of Sections 706(f) through 706(k), 42 U.S.C. 2000e–5(f)–(k), to bring this action.

5. At all relevant times, (name of defendant) has been a public entity as defined in Section 12131(1) of the ADA, 42 U.S.C. 12,131(1), in that it is a state or local governmental entity or agency thereof.

6. At all relevant times (name of defendant) has received federal funds.

7. Since at least (date), (name of defendant) has engaged in unlawful practices in violation of ADA Sections (list specific sections of Title II of the ADA that were violated) and in violation of Section 504 of the Rehabilitation Act, 42 U.S.C. 794. These practices include but are not limited to denying (name of plaintiff)—an individual with a disability who, with or without reasonable modifications to rules, policies, or practices; the removal of architectural, communication or transportation barriers; or the provision of auxiliary aids and services, meets the essential eligibility requirements for the receipt of services or the participation in programs or activities provided by (name of defendant's)—access to the (name of program, service or activity) of (name of defendant).

8. The effect of the practices complained of has been to deprive (name of plaintiff) equal access to a public entity's services, programs, and activities and to otherwise adversely affect his/her status as a member of the public interested in accessing (name of defendant)'s programs and activities.

Prayer for Relief

WHEREFORE, the plaintiff respectfully requests that this court:

A. Grant a permanent injunction enjoining (name of defendant), its owners, officers, management personnel, employees, agents, successors, assigns, and in participation with them, from engaging in discrimination based on disability in the programs, services, and activities of (name of defendant).

B. Order (name of defendant) to formulate and implement services, programs, and activities that provide equal access to otherwise qualified individuals with disabilities and to eradicate the effects of past and present unlawful practices in the carrying out of (name of defendant)'s programs, services, and activities.

C. Order (name of defendant) to make (name of plaintiff) whole by providing plaintiff with appropriate remuneration incurred in obtaining suitable programming, services, and activities, with prejudgment interest, in amounts to be proved at trial, and other affirmative relief necessary to eradicate the effects of its unlawful practices, including the making of reasonable modifications and the provision of auxiliary aids and services so that (name of plaintiff) can access the programs, services, and activities of (name of defendant).

D. Grant such further relief as the Court deems appropriate.

E. Grant the plaintiff his/her fees and costs in this action.

Jury Demand
Plaintiff demands trial by jury.

Title III Complaint
(Seeking injunctive relief for discrimination by a place of public accommodation)

Nature of Action
This is an action under Title III of the Americans with Disabilities Act of 1990 ("ADA") to enjoin unlawful disability-based discrimination. Plaintiff, (name of plaintiff), was discriminated against on the basis of disability so that he was denied the full and equal enjoyment of the goods, services, facilities, privileges, advantages, or accommodations of a place of public accommodation owned, leased, or operated by the defendants, (name of defendants).

Jurisdiction and Venue
1. Jurisdiction of this court is proper under 28 U.S.C. 451, 1331, 1337, and 1343. This action is brought under Section 12,188(a) of the ADA, 42 U.S.C. 12,188(a)—incorporating by reference the remedies and procedures found in 42 U.S.C. 2000a–3, Section 204 of the Civil Rights Act of 1964. [If architectural accessibility is involved, you may also want to consider pleading state law claims. It is not unusual for states to have even more strict architectural standards than those required by the

ADA. Also, plaintiff should consider suing the architect of the building directly for designing a building out of compliance with ADA architectural standards. Finally, defendant may want to consider suing the architect for malpractice.]

2. The alleged unlawful practices were and are now being committed in the _____ District of _____, _____ Division.

Parties

3. (Name of plaintiff) is a person with a disability, (state nature of disability), who was denied the full and equal enjoyment of the goods, services, facilities, privileges, advantages, or accommodations of a place of public accommodation owned, leased, or operated by the defendant.

4. Name of plaintiff is expressly authorized under Section 308 of the ADA, 42 U.S.C. 12,188(a)—incorporating by reference the remedies and procedures found in 42 U.S.C. 2000a–3, Section 204 of the Civil Rights Act of 1964—to bring this action.

5. At all relevant times (name of defendant A) has been the owner/ lessor of (location of the place of public accommodation).

6. At all relevant times (name of defendant B) has been the operator of (name of the place of public accommodation).

7. (Name of the place of public accommodation) at all relevant times has been a place of public accommodation in that it is a place of public accommodation under (select applicable type of public accommodation as set forth in 42 U.S.C. 12,181(7). Include its corresponding statutory reference).

Statement of Claims

8. Since at least (date), (names of all defendants) have engaged in unlawful practices in violation of ADA Sections (list specific sections of Title III of the ADA that were violated). These practices include but are not limited to (list the incidents of discrimination by each defendant).

9. The effect of the practices complained of has been to deprive (name of plaintiff) the full and equal enjoyment of a place of public accommodation and to otherwise adversely affect his/ her status as a member of the public interested in accessing the

place of public accommodation owned, leased, and/or operated by the defendants, (names of defendants).

Prayer for Relief

WHEREFORE, the plaintiff respectfully requests that this court:

A. Grant a permanent injunction enjoining (names of defendants), its officers, management personnel, employees, agents, successors, assigns, and in participation from engaging in discrimination based on disability.

B. Order (names of defendants) to make (name of place of public accommodation) readily accessible to and usable by individuals with disabilities.

C. Order defendants to provide the auxiliary aids, services, modify policies, or provide an alternative method so that (name of plaintiff) can obtain the full and equal enjoyment of the place of public accommodation, (name of place of public accommodation), owned, operated, or leased by defendants.

D. Grant the plaintiff his/her costs and reasonable attorney fees in this action.

NOTICE TO PRODUCE

Key

In a jurisdiction that adheres to the Revised Discovery Rules, much of what follows below is covered in the initial disclosures. In such jurisdictions, a lawyer commonly writes to his or her adversary before the scheduling conference listing the documents he or she expects in the disclosures. If the other side fails to furnish those documents, the lawyer then seeks judicial sanctions. Also, the notices to produce contained here are not meant to be specific to any of the titles of the ADA.

Plaintiff's Request to Produce

Pursuant to Rule 34, Plaintiff requests that the following documents be produced at the offices of _____, located at _____ on _____ _____, for the purpose of inspection and copying by the Plaintiff.

Definition: Disability—A person has a disability if he/she has a physical or mental impairment that substantially limits one or more of life's major activities; has a record of such an impairment; or is perceived as having such an impairment.

1. Any and all records analyzing the job tasks of the position held by the Plaintiff.
2. Any and all personnel records of Plaintiff.
3. Any and all records of Plaintiff kept in confidential files in accordance with federal law, such as pursuant to the Americans with Disabilities Act of 1990.
4. Any and all tests that Plaintiff took as part of the preemployment hiring process, including the actual test questions themselves.
5. The employment application filled out by Plaintiff.
6. The financial and annual reports of Defendant. (**Note:** This may not be discoverable unless the Defendant alleges that the accommodation would be an undue hardship.)
7. Defendant's employee handbook.
8. Defendant's 504/ADA Grievance Procedure.
9. Defendant's self-evaluation plan.
10. Defendant's transition plan.
11. Defendant's organizational chart.
12. Defendant's EEO reports for relevant years.
13. Any certifications by the head of the public entity of undue burden.
14. Any and all notes, documentation, or questions used during the exam performed on Plaintiff at Defendant's behest either while Plaintiff was in Defendant's employ or subsequent to a conditional job offer. Include the results and conclusions of said exam. (Be aware that the employer may not have anything other than conclusions.)
15. Plaintiff's job description.
16. Copies of the long- and short-term disability policies offered by the Defendant.
17. The actuarial data used to decide the limitation on (state disability at issue).

18. Copies of the collective bargaining agreement, relevant grievance files, amendments to the collective bargaining agreement, and the letter of agreement between the collective bargaining unit and the Defendant.

19. Any materials that describe the nature and scope of (name of program/activity/service at issue). Include any data or information indicating the nature of the population served by the program/activity or service at issue.

20. Any materials detailing the criteria for admission to the (list name of program/activity or service at issue).

21. Transcripts and minutes of the meeting of (date) in which the zoning of (state name of defendant's business) was discussed. Include the list of witnesses appearing at that meeting.

22. The architectural plans/blueprints for the building housing the place of public accommodation at issue.

23. Any architectural records, materials, documents sent to (name of state in which place of public accommodation is located) in accordance with (name of state in which place of public accommodation is located) equal access laws.

24. The architectural plans for the alterations performed at (location of place of public accommodation and place of public accommodation itself).

25. Any materials describing the nature and scope of the (name of place of public accommodation) business.

26. Copies of the lease between (name of place of public accommodation and its lessor).

27. The records of Defendant pertaining to the investigation of Plaintiff's physical/mental condition and the determination of coverage or noncoverage under (name of Defendant or Defendant's administrator of the disability plan) benefit/disability plans.

28. Any written materials, records or documents kept by Defendant in its benefits department pertaining to any medical care received by plaintiff while employed by Defendant.

29. Any and all records pertaining to Defendant's investigation of Plaintiff's physical/mental impairment.

30. The job description of the persons holding Plaintiff's position prior to and subsequent to plaintiff.

INTERROGATORIES

It may not be possible to ask all of these interrogatories, as many jurisdictions limit the amount of interrogatories that can be asked. Also, there may be standard language used for interrogatories.

Plaintiff's Interrogatories

The Plaintiff requests that the following interrogatories be answered under oath by Defendant.

Definitions:

Disability—A person has a disability if he/she has a physical or mental impairment that substantially limits one or more of life's major activities, has a record of such an impairment, or is perceived as having such an impairment.

Physical/Mental Condition—The Plaintiff's physical or mental status.

1. The name, title, and address of the officers of Defendant involved in the decision to restructure the company's health insurance plan.
2. The name, title, and address of the officers of Defendant that were responsible for compiling/overseeing any and all actuarial data justifying the distinction in benefit levels among disabilities.
3. Detail completely the investigation made by Defendant as to Plaintiff's physical/mental condition and coverage under the Defendant's benefits plan.
4. At any time, did the Defendant or its officers, employees, or agents receive any information as to the Plaintiff's physical/mental condition?
5. If Defendant did receive information about the Plaintiff's physical/mental condition, please state the nature of that information, its source, when that information was received, and where that information was kept.
6. Did the Defendant or its officers, employees, or agents receive any information as to the Plaintiff's physical/mental condition at any time during the course of Plaintiff's employment with Defendant? If so, please state the nature of that information

and its source. Also, describe where that information was stored by the Defendant.

7. Detail completely the investigation made by Defendant as to Plaintiff's physical/mental condition.

8. Identify the person answering these interrogatories.

9. Identify all individuals (part-time and full-time) who have worked under Plaintiff's supervisor for three years prior to and subsequent to Plaintiff's employ with defendant. Please provide the names and addresses of such persons.

10. Identify by name and address the individual hired into the vacancy sought by Plaintiff.

11. Describe in detail the reasons for selecting the individual hired for the vacancy sought by Plaintiff.

12. Describe in detail just how the Defendant determined the essential functions of Plaintiff's position/sought by Plaintiff.

13. State whether any person employed by Defendant has received any comment, criticism, or complaint concerning the Plaintiff's conduct or job performance.

14. If an employee of Defendant has received any comment, criticism, or complaint concerning the Plaintiff's conduct or job performance, provide the name, title, and address of such person.

15. If an employee of Defendant has received any comment, criticism, or complaint concerning the Plaintiff's conduct or job performance, state the specifics of the comment, complaint, or criticism.

16. If an employee of Defendant has received any comment, criticism, or complaint concerning the Plaintiff's conduct or job performance, identify the person making the comment, criticism, or complaint by name, employment, job title, and last known address.

17. If an employee of Defendant has received any comment, criticism, or complaint concerning the Plaintiff's conduct or job performance, identify the occasion for the making of such comment, criticism, or complaint.

18. Please describe whether the safety of the public, other employees, or the self was a fundamental aspect of the position held by Plaintiff while in Defendant's employ.

19. State the name, title, and address of all persons participating in the process of hiring the Plaintiff and describe the roles played by each.

20. Describe all instances where Defendant offered to make accommodations for Plaintiff's disability. Include in that description the name, title, and address of the person offering the accommodation. Also, include the date(s) the accommodation was offered and the specific accommodation offered, as well as whether such accommodations were accepted by Plaintiff.

21. Describe the purpose of the department Plaintiff worked in while in Defendant's employ and how that department relates to Defendant's company achieving its goals. Also, state the various locations where this department conducts operations.

22. Describe the operations of the department Plaintiff worked in while in Defendant's employ. Provide the name, title, and address of each person in that department.

23. Describe the preemployment hiring process. Include in that description the nature of any tests that applicants take in that process as well as the test and the test questions themselves.

24. Describe the medical exam performed on Plaintiff on _____ (date) while plaintiff was employed by Defendant. Include in that description the scope of such exam and the reasons for Defendant insisting on such an exam.

25. Did anyone in Defendant's employ encourage Plaintiff to seek SSI, long- or short-term disability benefits? If so, state the name, title, and address of such person.

26. Describe the _____ program/activity/service (Title II or III matter assumed). In that description, describe the purpose of the program/activity, the number of employees in that program/activity, the population served by the program/activity, the locations where the program/activity occurs, and whether such programs/activities are integrated with the nondisabled.

27. Describe the eligibility requirements for the _____ program/activity.

28. (public entity assumed) Does Defendant claim that accommodating Plaintiff would result in an undue burden? If so, please state when the head of Defendant certified as such (Title II assumed as to certification).

29. Describe the process for which an adverse zoning decision against Plaintiff was made.
30. When was Defendant's facility built?
31. Has Defendant's facility been altered or renovated since 1/26/92?
32. Is Defendant a religious entity? If so, describe.
33. Is Defendant's place of business under lease? If so, state the name and address of the lessor.

REQUEST TO ADMIT

Request to Admit can be a very useful tool to narrow the issues of contention. As for what to ask in a Request to Admit, refer to the Checklists, the Interrogatories, and the Notices to Produce. It is possible that useful Requests to Admit could be formulated based on that material.

Epilogue

I HOPED TO ACCOMPLISH SEVERAL goals with this book. First, the book needed to be comprehensively updated. Second, I wanted to make the Americans with Disabilities Act, as it exists today, understandable. Though the law is extremely comprehensive and complex, there is, in my opinion, unnecessary confusion and complexity. Thus, think of this book as a primer on how the ADA actually works—an ADA road map, if you will. Third, I wanted to show the reader just how broad the ADA really is. Fourth, I wanted to cover some of the recurring problems that I have seen over the years, decipher them in a manner that could be understood, and suggest ways to deal with the issues so that larger problems could be averted. I also wanted to focus on problems that have kept recurring since the first edition was written and eliminate from discussion anticipated problems that never came to pass. Fifth, I wanted to discuss ways that the ADA might evolve so that businesses could better plan for the future. Finally, I wanted people, after reading this book, to say to themselves, "I can work with this law," and not succumb to anti-ADA feelings that often exist. Of course, the book is no substitute for competent legal counsel.

Before signing off, let me say that writing the second edition of this book has been a pleasant, though time-consuming, obsession for me. Again, I have to thank my wife for suggesting and then encouraging me to undertake this. She was right; it was worth it. I do hope the reader shares my assessment that the rather ambitious goals I have set for this book have been accomplished. If not, I hope the reader has at least achieved a level of comfort for working with the ADA. The ADA is a good law, and now that readers are able to understand it and have some idea of how to work with it, perhaps it can achieve its promise of making the world a more accessible and better place for persons with disabilities.

William D. Goren

Table of Statutes and Regulations

References to page numbers alone are for instances when the case is mentioned in the text. References to a page number followed by an endnote number (n.#) are for instances when the case is cited in the endnotes but not the text.

Regulations

Statutes

Guidances

Table of Cases

References to page numbers alone are for instances when the case is mentioned in the text. References to a page number followed by an endnote number (n.#) are for instances when the case is cited in the endnotes but not the text.

Index

T

Title I, ADA
  mental retardation 116
  otherwise qualified 14
  regulations implementing 15
  sports, college and high school
    111
  sports, professional 104
Title II, ADA. *Also see* public sector
    14
  mental retardation 116
  otherwise qualified 14
  Rehabilitation Act of 1973,
    remedies under 97
  sports, college and high school
    111
Title III, ADA. *Also see* public
    accommodations, places of
  administrative remedies 98
  Internet 120–21
  mental retardation 116
  physical structures, limitations to
    120
  sports, college and high school
    111

U

U.S. Department of Justice 53, 60, 73,
    76, 97
undue burden
  mental retardation 117
  public accommodations, places of
    74
undue hardship 29-37
  EEOC definition of 29
  inconvenience, differentiated from
    30
  measurement of in workplace 30

W

worker's compensation 87
  essential functions of the job 87
  forbidden under the ADA 87
  full return to work after on-the-job
    injury 87
  history of, request for 87